How to Skin a Skunk

By the Same Author:

The Adventures of Nathaniel B. Oakes

Never Squeeze a Honeybee!
The Continuing Adventures of Nathaniel B. Oakes

How to Skin a Skunk

Even More Adventures of Nathaniel B. Oakes

Nathaniel B. Oakes

J.D. Oakes Publishing
Spokane, WA

Copyright © 2025 by Nathaniel B. Oakes

J.D. Oakes Publishing, Spokane, WA

www.jdaokes.com

Cover design and illustrations by Darren Cools

All rights reserved. No part of this book may be reproduced, stored in a retrieval system, or transmitted in any form, or by any means, electronic, mechanical, photocopying, or otherwise, without the prior written permission of the publisher, except by a reviewer, who may quote brief passages in a review.

Printed in the United States of America.

ISBN 978-0-9844832-7-3

Contents

Acknowledgements 7

Crack the Whip. 9

Of Baling Twine and Monkeyshine 18

Tree Fort Treasures. 24

Who Micky Moused This? 29

Frog Farm 33

The Deer Hunt 45

Sam 55

Racing 63

Badger Fight 71

Horse and Sleigh 76

Cars and Kids. 84

The Cows Are Out! 96

Noses and Toeses. 102

How to Skin a Skunk

Animal House 107

Pig Slop 116

Big Boots to Fill 121

See-Saw 124

Jumping Jehosaphat and All That 132

Down Under 136

Lookout Hike 139

Drowning Worms 146

Skunk Story 155

He Swallowed the Whole Thing! 161

Chickenpox 166

Skyhooks 170

Hay Stacking 174

Catching Crawdads 181

Climbing Trees 190

Acknowledgements

To my wife, through whose indefatigable will and God's grace, continues to tend and mend me and the children.

To my long suffering ediatrix, Suzanne Andres, who made a heroic attempt to keep me and Grammar in a friendly relationship.

And to Darren Cools, my principal illustrator with fifteen drawings and book cover.
Riley Mason-Schickel for five drawings. Draeksley Weston for his one; and finally, for collaborative drawings by David Cools, James Cools, Nathaniel Cools and Jonathan Cools.

Crack the Whip

Did you know that the tremendous cracking sound when a muleskinner cracks his whip at his stubborn mules is caused by the tip of the whip breaking the sound barrier as it whips around to come back at the skinner? Well, it is! That puts the speed of a whip tip at just over 701 miles per hour at sea level. Now our farm wasn't at sea level, it was about 2200 feet above, so perhaps a smidgeon more speed could be had by the tip before break speed. (A smidgeon is the third cousin of the pigeon, but much shyer, so you don't see him often). We didn't know the numbers then, but we felt them, and it's pretty darn fast.

You are doubtful. Well, I didn't say much over the speed of sound, just a smidgeon (there he is again, and he's getting bolder). I don't want to exaggerate, I would be careful not to overstate my case, but, say 706 miles per hour. Now that would seem just too much, but certainly 701.5 miles per hour rounded up to 702 would be reasonable?

And how did we manage to get to these remarkable speeds you may ask? Well. If you would have said cow, instead of how, you'd of gotten it right off. Yes, there were many times that we had to round up cranky cows, and to do this we had to get a rope around their necks and lead them to where they didn't want to go. Our farm was horseless, and so all the cowboy wannabe work was done from the ground, on foot.

First the cow had to be lassoed. You know, get a loop of rope around its neck. Do you know what cowboy lariats are? They're ropes that cowboys use to loop cows. Well, these ropes are so stiff that when they make a loop they look like the steel hoop of an old whiskey barrel. The cowboy just swings this stiff loop into the air, and it remains a perfect circle until it settles nicely over a cow's head and cowabunga! She's wearing a necktie.

This cowboy rope is so stiff he can just sorta roll it out there in front of the cow's feet and when she runs into the loop, she's hogtied. I've even seen a cowboy just cast a loop in under the belly of an escaping cow and she runs into it with her hind feet and *zip!* Her two hind legs are noosed together and she's caught.

Crack the Whip

Now she's a three legged cow. Yes, this is the kind of rope that Will Rogers could make stand up and dance, roll around and do tricks. Makes cowboying a whole lot easier when you have a rawhide rope with the spine of the cow still in it like they did.

Well, now that you know what those lariats are, we didn't have one. No, we had strong but spineless ropes. They couldn't hold a loop. You had to get up real close and try to flip a limp loop at the head of a cow as it tried to dart past and hope it catches it.

And no, I never tried to put salt on a bird's tail. Supposedly it's a lot easier to catch a bird if you salt his tail. Maybe it helps on pigs? Sailors eat a lot of salt pork. But to put salt on a steer's tail seemed a better idea when it's put on a platter at supper than when he's still on the hoof, so we just opted to catch cows the old fashioned way. Albeit with wimpy ropes.

Now to get close enough to have a chance of roping a rangy cow, we had to herd it by foot into a field corner. We accomplished this by forming a semi-circle of kids and slowly closing in on the cow until it was cornered. Trouble is, a cow knows when it's cornered and takes a mighty objection to it.

The biggest kid got the rope lassoing responsibility, and so it was his responsibility to fling the rope's limp loop over the head of the cow as it milled around in the pen made of human pickets. As you know, a chain is only as strong as its weakest link, and so too a fence is as strong as its weakest spot, and I guess the cow knew it too, 'cause that cow was always looking for a way to break past one of us kids.

How to Skin a Skunk

If it was really committed to breaking out of its confines, it required a split second decision whether to hold your ground as it charged, or stand firm and bluff it into thinking the quaking kid standing in its way was a solid post. If your bluff didn't work then you risked being trammeled into the ground as it ran over you. To leap out of the way too soon was to give the cow an easy break (and the distinct possibility that the epitaph "you're scared," might be aired), and it would never be caught if it knew that every time it ran at you it got away. No, you had to stand firm until your leap out of the way cost you a little skin. Perhaps a bruise or a little hair clutched in the hand might do.

And so, as it happened this time, Andy, Jake, Jeremy, Ivan, Peter, Tristan, and Damien and I had the task of catching the steer, Duke. Andy had the rope, about a twenty-five footer or more, so lots of kids could get a hold when the cow was lassoed and tried to run away.

Now Duke was a sizable steer even for his young age. He arrived into this world at a whopping 105 lbs, and now at 800 lbs he was well muscled and athletic. So when we cornered him, he didn't like it very much and looked for a way out. Good thing bovine brains are not made for thinking. How could an 800 lb steer not know that all he had to do was to run over any one of us pedestrian cowpunchers?

Reality had not quite kept up with our bragging, as none of us had actually body slammed a steer into the ground, and as the battle lines were drawn this time, it didn't seem a likely outcome. And it wasn't. He escaped three times from the semicircle by rushing the gap between us. It wasn't without recriminations though; they flew fast and furious.

"Why didn't you stop him?" "Well, don't run AWAY from where he's going!" "Run INTO the gap!" "You can't let them know you're afraid of em." "Next time, everybody move up closer so it looks like there're smaller gaps."

This was all spoken bravely from the cowboy farthest from the prowling steer. Forty-five minutes later we once again chased him around the field until we had him cornered.

This time he ran past Andy, who had the rope, and was able to flip it over the steer's head while it shot the gap between him and Jake. As Andy was jerked nearly off his feet, it was incumbent that everybody else grab the rope and exert enough drag before the steer could get up to real speed. If he did, Andy would have been a goner. The steer could run much faster and would fling Andy off his feet.

And the fun began. We all lunged for the rope from whatever angle we came flying in. Jake was the closest, and so he managed to grab the tailing rope when some of it was still in the air behind Andy. The rest of us had to grab the remaining rope as it sped along the ground trailing Andy and Jake. Amidst their hollering "Grab the rope! Grab the rope!" were the squeals and grunts of the rest of us trying to grab a rope that slithered along the ground, while at the same time we were doubled over and running.

Although we provided comedic entertainment for the rest of the farm stock, it was serious business for us. Who wanted to go chasing all over the field trying to corner this beast again? So we all lunged and grabbed the rope as well as we could. Jeremy managed to catch hold while still on his feet but was jerked unceremoniously OFF his feet as soon as he stood up. The cow jerked the rope from his hands and took a little skin with it. I dove and clutched the rope. Jerked forward, I shot out of my shoes and toppled forward onto my belly from whence I was dragged.

Now some of you have been dragged through a cow pasture by a fleeing steer, and some of you haven't. But that doesn't make any difference to the boy it's happening to now just as it didn't help me then. Because at this moment I was trying to keep my chin from bouncing up and down on the ground, by craning my neck up as far as I could, while my arms, stretched straight out in front of me, were nearly out of their sockets.

This stopped the chin dance but little else. Vetch vines, grass shoots, and a world of weeds all smacked me in the face and then began to fill up my shirt as they squeezed eagerly under my collar. My belt buckle scraped into the ground and threatened to fill my pants with ants and other sordid insect relatives. For a fleet second my bobbling eyes spotted a Praying Mantis as it dropped to its knees in desperate prayer. "Deliver this thy prostrate child that he may not return to earth from whence he came but by the aid of his soles departed he might become upright again and run very firma upon the terra."

Well it did some good; Jeremy was able to regain his balance and managed to catch up as the steer swung heavily to the left, thus decelerating the end of the rope for a few seconds just as

Crack the Whip

Andy and Jake were losing the battle to slow the steer down. A cause for celebration for sure, and I like pies as well as the next guy, but I was very concerned about the cow pies coming at me fast and furious now. I swung my head desperately from one side to the other to avoid getting one smacked in my face or getting greased from head to toe as I was being dragged through one, so when the steer turned sharply, I took immediate advantage of it and leapt to my feet. Peter, Tristan and Damien had been in hot pursuit and here joined the team. So the steer, having turned and slowed the forward movement, now shot ahead with a will, trying to break free of the weight around his neck. This straightened the rope rapidly, and we were snapped into a straight line behind him.

With all of us finally tagged on, our weight was nearing his, and if we could just keep our feet under us we might be able to slow him down. We were running at breakneck speed as he commenced to try to outrun us so we would be forced to let go, and indeed we already had to let go with one hand just to keep our balance. What a sight we made! We tried to run fast enough not to get pulled over, at the same time trying to pull backwards to drag on the rope and tire the steer out so he would slow down and stop. This required our taking long stiff legged steps, with one hand clutching the rope and the other twirling like a windmill in a desperate attempt to stay balanced.

And then that wily steer stirred things up. He veered sharply to the right, thus flinging us to the left. Then just when he'd lurched in that direction, he turned sharply to the left and thrust us to right, but at startling speeds. Yes, like the cracking of a whip. First to the right we went at 30 miles an hour, then to the left nearing 60. To the right again and pushing 90.

Now the flinging and the flung had begun. Peter was flung when whipped to the left, and landed on his hinder and skidded across the pasture with his tailbone playing jackhammer as he went. Damien went next. He fared better as he left us. His grip torn from the rope but the rest of him staying upright, he went shooting across the pasture with both arms twirling like windmills into the distance. Tristan followed by being on the wrong side of the rope. It clipped him to the ground, knocking his wind out. And now, doggone, if that steer didn't whip to the right again. The speed at the end increased exponentially, just where Jeremy and I were.

With one arm stuck to the rope and the other swinging wildly, Crack! We were shot off the end of the rope. It was way too speedy for our unfortunate legs. They went as fast as they could, but our tops went faster, and over we went face first. Jeremy, always the athlete, managed to roll head over heels at a dizzying rate, coming to a stop in time to observe Andy and Jake still hanging on, dragged on their feet like skiers as the wearing out steer began to slow. As for me, I was back to belly flop. Whump! Out went my air. Once again, I skidded across the pasture on my stomach. Once again, the pasture tried to fill my clothes just where the last run had joggled out the dirt and weeds, ants and perhaps their uncles. The drag of the earth stopped me and I gasped to regain my breath.

Crack the Whip

I'm sure we must have reached the sound barrier. I heard the Crack! Jeremy heard the Crack! Or perhaps it was our necks that cracked as we were snapped around at the end of the rope. Likely we broke the sound barrier a smidgen, as that shy little fellow just popped back into my story!

Anyways we all got up and ran to give Andy and Jake a hand as they tried to drag the steer where he didn't want to go. The steer had tired a bit, and so we were able to once again grab the rope and bring the steer to a stand still.

You're welcome to grab a hold of the rope and help out next time. It can whip mighty quick though, maybe even into the next tale.

Of Baling Twine and Monkeyshine

I stood there, pondering, figuring, cocking my head this way and the other, stroking my chin; the beard had many more months to wait before it was out and about ready to be stroked, but I tried.

I was four years old as I watched Daddy unroll a tan colored rubber like tube with a flange running the whole twenty foot length of it. He was at the front door. The front door was wide open, and he began to nail this flange to the doorjamb, starting at the bottom and working his way up, but, nope, as I watched I couldn't figure out what it was.

"What is that?" I asked Daddy as he tapped away with his small hammer. He was on his knees and turned his face to mine to answer, "Monkeyshine." "Monkeyshine?" "Yes," he continued at my quizzical look. "You just put it around the whole doorjamb in the groove, and when you close the door no cold air can get in. It seals the door up. See? Monkeyshine."

Well I guess I saw. Monkeyshine. Hmmmmm. In my four years I hadn't been able to traverse my whole brain yet, but I kept trying, and no, I hadn't heard of Monkeyshine. But then again maybe it wasn't that important to get it all figured out. The smile that played around Daddy's eyes betrayed him. It gave away just enough to let me know that he was funning, and left just enough mystery to make it fun.

But goodness. This could get confusing. Wasn't that a can of Monkeyshine that Dad had squirt into the door hinges of the car to keep it from squeaking? Seems I remember asking the same question when he was applying this to the car. "What's that?" I asked. This philosophical life begins in wonder and ends in wisdom if one can apply his mind well, and I was getting late to the game at four.

"Monkeyshine," came the answer, his back to me. But when he turned around there was that glint in his eye again.

And wasn't that Monkeyshine that Leo waxed his bow string with? I especially remember me, or was it myself, it's so long ago

How to Skin a Skunk

I can't remember, watching a bit perplexed as Leo rubbed a bar of paraffin wax up and down the bow string and I asked in the most serious manner, "What's that?" Sure enough the answer was "Monkeyshine."

Strangely, the older I got, the more Monkeyshine disappeared from the farm.

So it was with baling twine. It slowly disappeared as plastic rope replaced hemp. But what is baling twine?

Well, a bale of hay is a very compacted bunch of alfalfa or grass, compacted by a machine called, of course a baler. The baler was pulled by a tractor and it swathed up a windrow of loose hay into its maw and out from the back toppled a solid bale of hay weighing anywhere from sixty to a hundred pounds, cast to the ground. Now what kept this loose hay compacted were two strings that went around the rectangle of hay, knotted fast so the compacted hay could not spring apart. The string was called twine, hence baling twine. In those days this twine was made from hemp, a plant that has a very sinuous stem when the fibers are extracted and twisted together to form a rope or thick twine. It was tan in color.

Once it was relieved from its duty as a binder for a bale, baling twine was put to work for practically everything that needed binding. We would cut it from the bale and drape it over a nail or post or stuff it into a burlap grain sack until we needed its services.

Our tree forts were held up with baling twine. We would latch the cross poles for the floor between trees with cords of baling twine, then latch all the floor poles to these to make the

Of Baling Twine and Monkeyshine

floor. Then we latched more poles up higher for railings. Jeremy's fort about twelve feet up even sported a roof with lashed poles. Andy's was up twenty feet with a roof and all the construction held together by yards and yards of hemp rope. The hemp was very biodegradable though, and it rotted quite quickly when left in the weather. To climb up the ladders to the forts a few months after they had been lashed could be a hairy experience. A rope would break and a rung would give way and you dangled a moment until you caught another rung that didn't give way. So it was that inspections were needed to be assured that tween this time and that time, your twine was fine.

Setting up corrals for the cows was another work this rope was put to. Not real permanent corrals, or nails or wire would be used. Rope would rot too fast. But for quick temporary pens of a few months use, baling twine was your answer.

One day Jake got a splendid idea for making a climbing rope. First he braided three strands of rope together. This braiding was standard practice for us to make throwing ropes, hauling ropes, and suchlike, that would be very strong all braided together. This time, though, Jake and Jeremy braided the three and took three such braided ones and braided them together. I think they did another round too, ending up with a very thick strong rope which in length was about twenty five feet. They then shimmied up two trees that grew about ten feet apart and lashed a stout pole across with more twine. From the middle of the beam they hung the climbing rope.

We had a great time then, seeing who could climb the highest. I don't remember getting very far up. Leo, Andy, Jake and

How to Skin a Skunk

Jeremy could make it up to touch the beam, by wrapping their legs in the rope as they pulled up with arms and pushed with legs.

One day in the late afternoon we bantered about as follows.

Colonel Stringbean to Chief Little Muscles: "But we should let Plump Woman try."

Chief Little Muscles, worried: "But the rope might not be strong enough." He looked for me. The rope nearly hid me completely. My weight could hardly even have straightened the curves out of the rope.

President Blockhead proposed that Captain Floodpants might be a good candidate since his pants were already higher up so he would have less distance to climb, but that was vetoed by Chief Little Muscles as his biceps were clearly visible and there was flesh on the forearms. I thought that Colonel Stringbean should have a go, as a string is as good as a rope, being as a rope is very next of kin, and we might be able to upbraid him all the way up to the top.

So you see, really intelligent conversation was going on when Jake came out to the woods and climbed up. Just as he did so, Dad came walking toward us with an approving look.

As Jake caught his breath, Dad looked up the rope to the top and asked, "Mind if I try?" And as effortlessly as I am writing this down, Dad grasped the rope high up with his hands, raised his feet straight out perpendicular to the rope, pointed his toes enwrapped in his work boots, and climbed straight up to the top, arm over arm and right back down. Took a minute to pop our eyes back in their sockets as we were limp with astonishment and could hardly move. Wow! Few athletes can do that. And this was our Dad, who had just gotten home after a hard day's work in the fiery rooms of an aluminum smelter plant. And here we were, young bloods. Jake had some muscle, Jeremy did, mine were more anticipation than fact and had a hard time fighting off tame caterpillars, but we could only imitate firemen hugging their fire poles when we tried to climb. And here was Dad using arms alone, his legs straight out, climbing right up!

Now it is true, if I hadn't told you before, that he held his high school's Pole Vaulting record at Mount Carmel in Los Angeles for the bamboo pole. Very shortly thereafter, fiberglass replaced bamboo as pole material and a whole new era and technology of pole vaulting took over. Even so, the overall height record was broken only years later with these new poles.

As you see, Dad was not a newcomer to athletics, but he was, compared to us, an old comer and hadn't touched a pole vault or a climbing rope for thirty years or more. We just stood awe struck at what we saw. Dad with his usual diffidence smiled a little and told us some stories of playing around with the gym equipment with his chums at school. With that he left us. And then and there, two generations were bound together by a common bond none other than hemp rope baling twine.

Perhaps your home is as happy as mine, being held together with baling twine and monkeyshine? I sure hope so!

Tree Fort Treasures

I just don't understand anthropologists, those strange men who descended from ants so many centuries ago. I mean, they swarm all over ancient caves, dank jungles and burning deserts trying to discover how ancient men lived and how similar they might be to us now. They look all through old caves, stucco and stone houses for clues. If only they looked where the real treasures were hidden, in the ancient boys' tree houses.

Tree Fort Treasures

I think those old boys were pretty much like us. Each family brought into the world a passel or perhaps a passel and a half of boys. And those boys would have done what most boys do. They would have built tree houses. And sallying forth from those tree houses they would have found many adventures. So if those anthropologists really want to know how people lived they should go outside of all those old dwellings and find the old tree houses about a hundred to five hundred feet away. These were the dwellings that housed all the treasures worth discovering.

Oops! I probably shouldn't have mentioned that. Soon we'll have headlines screaming, "The inestimable John T. Hicklenstroper discovered the first known tree fort outside the ancient Greek ruins of Papadoulasphon, a city so ancient we don't yet know how to spell it. It was proved to be such when, as buried in the ground (well where else would it be buried?) a petrified tree with oodles of rings was found, and on that tree there was a sign with words written in an ancient and indecipherable code: "NO GIRLS ALLOWED!"

I don't know much about how trees get petrified so I can't tell their stories. But I bet almost all, except for a few deprived boys who never had tree forts, know how boys get petrified. The ancient story goes like this:

When a boy has resolved to sleep outside in his tree fort by himself, and has taken his resolution to that extreme juncture where he actually attempts it, and said boy is in fact laying in that tree fort at night, and furthermore that said boy is besought with a very vivid imagination, the ingredients are there for the process of petrifaction. The tree is an innocent bystander. Sometimes the process is not perfect. This is when there has not been quite enough terrification. Terrification can of course cause putrefaction, but that can be remedied by a quick trip to the privy.

Now when the aforesaid boy is buried in six feet of blankets up in his tree fort, and a hoot owl screeches in his ear, this causes terrification. This terrification can lead very quickly into petrifaction, like the time I was so petrified I couldn't move.

Or it can come in stages, like the time I was so terrified I just lay there for a second. As my supercharged imagination fleshed out the screech into a hairy tree wolf about to devour me, my legs began to move and I began to run.

"What's a tree wolf?" you ask. You ask that now?!!! You don't ask that kind of question until you're safe.

As my legs picked up speed I realized I had been running in place. I was still under the blankets. Good thing too. If I had been running standing up, I'd have run right over the edge of the tree fort. As it were, I leapt out of my covers just a couple of steps to the ladder, stepped and missed the rungs. Instead I grabbed the trunk of the tree with my fingers and toes and slid down it at a frightful rate. My finger and toenails left grooves in the bark as they tried to ease the fall. As I hit the ground, the hoot owl screeched another of its banshee like noises and terrrification hardened towards petrifaction. The blood began to freeze in my veins, my legs became rubbery and wouldn't move. The scream I had pent up so explosively wouldn't come out. I was now stiff with fright. "Petrifaction."

Tree Fort Treasures

The reason the anthropologist doesn't find petrified boys is that they have brothers and friends that come to chide them and laugh at them for being such a coward. This warms the blood back up very quickly, perhaps even to boiling, but that's evaporation and that's another story.

But back to tree forts and treasures. Tree forts hold treasures that any anthropologist, historian, paleontologist, or humorist would find most valuable. Archeologists could dig there with merit, as could just about any 'gist that just wanted to have a look.

To look into my tree fort treasures, let's start with skeletons. Wait! Wait! Come back! I don't have any skeletons that were in your closet. I don't even have any bipeds excepting birds: Robin, Sparrow, Starling, etc. See, the ornithologist is showing interest in this little box, in that one, and in this envelope. Now here is a chipmunk, a ground squirrel, and a skunk skull. Remember the skunk I picked up and skinned? You don't? Of course not! I haven't told you yet.

How about these birds' eggs? Look at this nice blue one. A robin egg. This speckled white is a killdeer. This little white one is a swallow's. And now don't laugh, but this is a pullet egg.

I was in third grade when I was given this egg by a friend of mine. He lived way up north of us, and I felt very special to have an egg from near Canada and from a bird I'd never heard of. Have you heard of a pullet?

Well I treasured that little brown egg for months until I got Marisa to look up in her books what a pullet bird is, and she had the unpleasant task of informing me that a pullet is none other than a young female chicken who hasn't got laying right yet and lays these sorry little eggs. I was crestfallen at the news, but I kept that little egg anyway because it still had curiosity value. Such a pathetic looking little thing for a chicken egg.

In the bottom of the box the treasures are a little more organized (for a boy that is), so let's dig into this assortment. A rusted fork with a tooth missing. Probably the one Davy Crocket used at the Alamo and a Mexican's bullet shot it off. A few old bullet shells, and here's one with the bullet still in it, turning green from the deteriorating copper casing. The one Custer probably wished he'd had but I have. Here's some silica rocks, so clear they look like ice chunks. An old pocket watch, broken. A completely rusted out pocket knife that must have graced the pocket of a pocket gopher for years under ground and not the pocket of a boy where it belonged. Ah, here's the first tooth I lost. Well, you get the picture.

We all had our treasure boxes secured in our tree forts, where we could store our finds gathered from adventuring. On listless summer days we could shimmy up the ladders to our forts, break open the treasure box, and finger all the precious artifacts.

Make sure you keep your treasure box safe, in your tree fort at best, in the basement if you must. Try not to lose it. Otherwise years from now an archeologist, paleontologist, or a philologist interested in the first letter you got from your fourth grade girlfriend will find it under a petrified tree and you don't want just any ol' 'gist running through your treasures. Gist saying....

Who Micky Moused This?

Since I never grew up with a T.V., I never saw the Mickey Mouse Show, and I'm quite certain to this day that I've never watched an actual episode of it. I have seen some of his Disney cartoons but that has been the extent of my association with Mickey Mouse on the screen.

It was off screen that my relationship with him was established. It was a strange relationship because I never saw Mickey Mouse in person nor even in mousen.

"Nathaniel," Daddy asked, "Could you hand me that ⅜-inch N wrench?" He would be holding some part of the engine of the car trying to put it back. "No, not that one, the one with the open end that has a three over a line with an eight below it." He could see into the toolbox from where he lay draped over the front fender, and from there he was trying to guide me to the correct wrench. As I was only six years old, this was not always easy. "No. No over to the left. No, that's your right. The other way. There, now put your hand straight down. "Yes, that one." And then, "Thank you," as I handed him his wrench. And in came Mickey Mouse.

Perhaps he was trying to put a new fuel pump in to replace an old one, but whatever it was, it was giving Dad trouble. I couldn't see over the fender, but it was obvious that whatever he was trying to fit into place just wasn't having it. After a furious struggle, he finally straightened up, flipped and caught the wrench in the air, looked down into the car where he had been working, and exclaimed, "Now who in the world Mickey Moused this thing together?"

Now how did an adjective and noun become a verb? How, in fact did Mickey Mouse become a verb? Even a kid like me knew that nouns can't be actions. They can have action but can't be one. Only verbs can move. A noun isn't an action, it's only a person, place or thing. The verbs are the action. Hold on. Did I say only verbs can move? That's not right. A verb can't move, only things can. Wow, this is getting confusing. You'd better call a grammarian quick because somebody might get hurt. Mickey Mouse is already getting all beat up.

Who did you imagine when Daddy said, "Who Mickey Moused this thing together?" Detroit? I didn't know yet that a

Who Micky Moused This?

place called Detroit was where they made oodles of cars. I didn't even know what an oodle was. You can cross a poodle with a noodle perhaps to get an oodle. But I didn't know that then, and I still don't know now. So it might have been Oodle cars that Detroit was Mickey Mousing together that had Dad so upset.

So it was that Mickey Mouse showed up a lot on our farm when fixing things was in season, especially where Dad was working.

As Dad struggled to get the nut off the bolt head because there wasn't room to get it at the right angle, "Well, of all the Mickey Moused ways of putting this thing together," he would say in disgust. I could see, in some ephemeral way, Mickey Mouse down in the engine causing trouble.

This image was etched in my mind more firmly as I heard Dad tell Mom he couldn't get the car fixed yet, as some knucklehead had Mickey Moused the parts together, and he had to figure out some way to get them off. Poor Mickey Mouse.

He came in handy sometimes though. Not the knucklehead, but Mickey Mouse. Our bike chains would break all too frequently as we sped about. To properly repair one, we needed a special link bought at a bike supply store. Of course we didn't have these little links on hand when we needed our steel steeds in action fast. So we had to Mickey Mouse the chain together with a cut off sixteen penny nail.

"Do you have a cotter pin to put in here?" a frustrated bike boy would ask. "The other one broke while I was removing it and now I can't get this to stay together."

"No, you'll just have to Mickey Mouse it together until we can get one." A nail or a strong piece of wire was typically used to do the Mickey Mousing.

Or, "The bolt holding these two do-dads together [do-dads are those things with names you don't remember] vibrated loose and was lost. Can you get me another?"

"I'll look, but you'll probably just have to Mickey Mouse it together for now."

These temporary repairs were never intended to become permanent fixtures. But like so many things in life, they did, and so they were still there years later when another unfortunate mechanic had to repair the same thing. You can hear him, as he shakes his head and mutters furiously, "Who in the heck Mickey Moused this thing together?" And sure enough there would be Mickey Mouse, years later, holding the same together.

Poor Mickey Mouse. He got called into service when needed, and then lost his name to derision when something went wrong.

And thus it was that Mickey Mouse popped up around our farm so many times. Always just out of sight, but responsible for so much.

Frog Farm

I liked frogs, and so did Jeremy. With most things we liked, if we could, we brought them home, and frogs were not excepted. They even topped our list, as the ponds in the old quarry behind our place provided us with an almost unlimited supply.

First, after the frogs started singing in the spring, came the polliwogs. We waited for the big, clear, gelatinous mass that held the little black frog eggs throughout it. Then, the teeny little polliwogs turned from eggs to tiny moving creatures. Then they grew bigger as they swam around like little fish. And, after a time, as if by magic, little hind legs would appear. With a wait of a few more days, out grew front legs, and they looked like fish with legs. And then quite suddenly the ponds were seething with little frogs. Having grown out of their tails and lost the gills for lungs, they were now just little frogs fit for Frog Pond School, not mere polliwogs anymore.

Not tadpoles either. Can you believe that some folks call polliwogs tadpoles? Well I can't either. They do though. At least Noah Webster thinks they do. He listened to every person that ever lived and wrote down all the words they said and he says they say tadpole. Says that the tad means toad, and the pol means head. So, you get a little feller called a tadpole.

Well. That's not poetic. No romance to the word. Now polliwog, see, comes from "pol" which means head, as we saw before, and "wog" for wriggle. Hence a wiggle head. And that's cute and that's a baby frog, not a toad. Knowing the difference between frogs and toads can be consequential as you shall find out.

Can you imagine if two grownups got married, and she was of the Polliwog persuasion, and he of the Tadpole? It couldn't be good. If you don't agree on Religion, Politics, and Polliwogs, you are in trouble. Could end up in the wedding banns. It landed me in trouble. Hop into the future and I will tell you how.

Frog Farm

Here was I, a college student. A little college snuggled in the hills of Southern California. A little Catholic one. Well not a little Catholic. A lot Catholic. But a little college. It wasn't Catholic just because it was universal to all the races there. No, it went further. It hosted a frog race. One I didn't know of until….

"I caught a frog! I caught a frog!" my girl exclaimed as she ran up to me with a little jar wherein sat a very disconsolate little toad. Well, how would you feel if you were unceremoniously snatched off your toadstool, cast into a jar, and the lid clamped shut? And then the snatcher shouted out to the world that you were a frog!? With the very real possibility that in her excitement she might kiss you?!

Well, this little fella had heard of his cousins the frogs being kissed by girls and turned into princes, but never toads. What would he become? What if he became a pauper instead of a prince? What to do? After all, as Shakespeare said, "Life is but a stage…."

How to Skin a Skunk

To which this snatched toad said, "Here I am in this drama and I will do my best." So, he tucked his little toad hands under his belly and his little toad feet under his hinder and attempted to look as froggy as he could.

Now my girl was a city girl born and bred, and just the fact that she could overcome her squeamishness and capture this little feller on her own was a huge accomplishment. I couldn't go and deflate her enthusiasm, especially since she was my sweetheart, and you don't go around insulting your sweetie unless you want her to go and start kissing frogs until she gets another prince.

So, I enthused as well as I could and congratulated her on her find, but it made my conscience jumpy. You see, when she had caught this little hopper to enter him into a frog race, she envisioned the frog prince statue reigning in splendor on her dorm room shelf. She thought that she had a frog. But I could see, being myself country born and bred, that this here little guy was a fraud, not a genuine frog. No, he was a toad. A little one sure, not like the huge, fat ones, but a frog fraud for sure.

But she didn't know this, and I don't think anyone else on the campus knew either. But I did. Now with her jumping around with excitement and me a bit perplexed as to what to do, I proffered a suggestion.

"Your frog is not a frog but a toad."

It didn't work. I could see the consternation begin to furrow her brow. I could see my love could be shattered against the very rocks that I eagerly would turn over to discover frogs. If I was going to try to turn her frog find into a frog fraud, I was in trouble.

Frog Farm

What you might not know, but I do, is that frogs and toads don't move about the same. Frogs hop almost exclusively, and toads walk. Maybe not all the way to Necedah, Wisconsin. Perhaps they may hop a train or catch a bus for all that, but to Tehachapi and back certainly. Toads tend to stroll about, ambulate, crawl, but seldom, if ever, do they simply hop. Sometimes faster, sometimes slower, but when they want to get somewhere, they just start walking. Especially young toads. They just set into it and then they are off. Now the big toads, the big fat ones that youngsters tend to hold up as trophies to unsuspecting mothers, do walk, but like their counterparts in the people population, as they get older and bigger, their walk becomes merely ambulatory, no zest.

So, here's the thing: Frogs hop and toads walk.

Frogs just hop when they want to hop. And when they hop, it may or may not be when you want them to hop. They may hop now or they may hop hours from now. There are times when they hop and then stop and then not hop. When they are in a race, you want them to hop, not stop, and then hop again, and keep on hopping until you want them to stop. Dr. Seuss tells when to stop the hop on Pop but is silent here. But here we want them to hop and not stop until they stop outside the prescribed circle.

Our frog race was set up like this: A big circle was to be circumscribed on the ground and the center of the circle marked. The contestants were to bring their frogs, and when the race was to begin, the judges would have all the contestants plop their frogs out of their frog containers into the center of the circle.

Whosever's frog hopped outside the circumference of the circle first was the winner.

Now I know that frogs in fright usually freeze and play dead. They need some incentive to hop. Sometimes the sight of a bush or a pond will incite them to try to get themselves to safety and they will begin to hop thataway. But I knew that there would be, surrounding the circle, a crowd of yelling and screaming alums, and most frogs would just freeze in fright. It's true, there might be some more boldly disposed frogs that would see a pretty face in the crowd and hop there for a hug in the hopes of getting a kiss and becoming a prince to have and to hold, but usually for a frog you have to poke him with a little prod if he's not hoppy happy.

So, I figured that most frogs would just sit there until they decided to hop, and usually if they did hop, they would not continue to do so. Thus, it would take the contestants a while to get their frogs jumping out of that circle. On the other hand, I knew almost for certain that once that toad was plopped out of his jar and into a tangle of frogs, surrounded by a bunch of cheering fans, he would run for cover. Well, perhaps he might not actually run, as galloping toads are not a common sight, but he would certainly walk right out of there with a will.

What was I to do? I didn't want to lose my girl by turning her frog into a toad. Yet I didn't want to have her win by a fraud, that wouldn't be fair to the other frog princesses. So, I hied to the judges and lifted my burdened conscience to them. Well, not one of them knew the difference between a toad and a frog and when they had put the contest together, they just figured that if it

Frog Farm

hopped it was a frog. Although even they knew that grasshoppers may not apply. Nor froghoppers or kangaroos. They didn't think anyone would know the frog/toad problem either and if they did, it would make a good laugh, so they just let her enter it right in.

So, I kept my secret to myself and looked eagerly forward to the race. Although, admittedly, a little cloud cast a shadow over my enthusiasm. What if her toad were to win? Would she kiss the toad? Now kissing a frog would already be fraught with danger. I did not want a handsome prince to pop up. But to kiss a toad?

I was nearly as discombobulated as the toad was. What if she won and kissed it?

A circle was drawn, about eight feet in diameter. The center was marked. The frog fanciers were called.

What was this? My sweetheart carrying the toad! A greenish, gray brown toad? Now I know I shouldn't be harsh on another's looks but I was a bit yellow with jealousy myself and so it might have colored my judgment. One couldn't really call him handsome, could he? After all he was a toad. This small feminine city girl carrying a toad? In her hand? Had he bewitched her with his toady ways, warts and all? What beguilements had the toad cast upon my girl to so turn her affections?

A bit astonished, I elbowed my way up to the forefront of the crowd of eds and co-eds to the circumference of the circle and took my place.

What did I wish for? To see this little fraud win? Or lose? If he won, I risked losing to a toad whatever he might turn into. If he lost, she would be so disappointed, and I certainly did not want to see a sad face. The dashed hope. A lost frog race could very well dash the hopes of fame and fortune or even a footnote in the mediocrity press.

Well the judge counted his one, two, three, and then said, "Go!" All the frog handlers rushed into the circle and dumped, plunked or plopped their little froggy friends into the center. My sweetheart gently set hers down amidst the fray. There were about twenty frogs in all.

This was enough to make the big crowd of students erupt into a rousing din as each voice joined the others in rooting for their favored frog, urging him to the finish. I added my husky cheers to help propel her toad to victory. Yes, I couldn't help it. I wanted to win. That toad had now become my own. And my fortune good or bad rested on it. My cries were lusty and loud as any as I yelled, "Go! Go!" And go he did.

He only paused a very short time, to get his bearings I suppose, and then he was off. He just looked straight ahead where he was pointed when she placed him and he began to walk. He just walked and walked and didn't stop until he walked right over that line. We were yelling, "Go! Go!" And he went, went. Right into the history books. There wasn't even a frog close. Oh, some of them did hop. Some hopped. Some sat. And most that did hop stopped. And the one that did hop a lot still stopped a lot between the hops. But the toad just walked and kept on walking and made up the ground between the frog hops and then a bit more ground when the hopping frog stopped. And … Well, you know, he won!

Frog Farm

And so, to this day there is a girl who has on her shelf a frog trophy on account of having won a frog race by the talents of a toad. And I was the biggest winner. I didn't have to tell her. She just couldn't get herself to kiss a toad however he had won such honors for her. And I, well, perhaps, maybe she might kiss me?

So you see you just have to know your toads and frogs.

And we better get back to frog farming where we left off before going into the future, and blast back to the past fast. Whew!

As I was saying these little polliwogs became frogs and we loved it. Jeremy and I built our frog pens, down by the old truck, the old '36 Chevy flatbed, along the timber line. The pens were about two feet by three feet, and built of wood. We just cobbled a bunch of old boards together with used nails. Inside we dug small holes into the ground and filled them with water. We found that that didn't work as the water just soaked into the earth. So we put old tuna or sardine cans in the holes and made little ponds that way.

The baby frogs were barely bigger than our thumbnails and looked cuter than a bug's ear when perched thereon. We built little wooden boxes and tunnels for them to hide in or crawl about. We would collect ten or more of these little creatures and put them in. With walls about eighteen inches high, we thought they would never escape. We had to learn the hard way that a frog is hard to keep penned in. They can virtually climb up just about anything, even glass. So they escaped practically as fast as we could put them in. We even built tight fitting lids after we discovered they could crawl right up the walls and out. These just slowed them down. We could never keep any of our batches of frogs in for more than a few days. We patched every hole and cranny to no avail.

We sure had fun trying, though the frogs gained a few names that were not very scientific but descriptive nonetheless. There is practically nothing cuter than having a frog sit on the end of your finger and look you straight in the face from his perch.

Even our sisters didn't mind our frogs so much. As long as their sporadic hops didn't land them on the girls, they thought the frogs were kind of cute too.

Most of these little frogs were green. Dark to pea and everything in between. Some were gray with black markings. But most unusual of all were orange or white ones. One out of two hundred or so would be orange and they were treasured because of their uniqueness. The white ones I suppose were albinos and we figured the orange ones were some variation of that. Perhaps blushing albinos?

One thing, though, we couldn't get Mom to like frogs. It's true she was a city girl from Los Angeles but she said she'd had a box turtle in a pen in her back yard that her brother Luis built for her. She would feed it lettuce and other turtle treats. But somehow she just couldn't stand frog grins. Even the orange ones couldn't melt her heart. In fact she just could not abide frogs at all.

Although she couldn't abide them, that didn't deter them from trying to abode with her. Why the frogs would try to come

Frog Farm

into our house I don't know. But sure enough throughout the summer a frog would show up in the home somewhere. And usually when Mom was alone. This did not bode well with the frog. You see, if it were one of the boys who ejected the frog from the premises we would pick him up and play with him until we went and placed him outside. Not so Mom. She would briskly flick him across the floor with the corn husk broom until he was dispatched through the open door. A curt, "And stay out!" often followed him.

But her favorite way was to capture it under an empty tuna or tomato can and then leave it there until one of us could throw it out. One time she clamped a can over a frog right when he tried to hop. In doing so, he left one hind foot behind and this foot was caught between the edge of the can and floor as she clamped down. So there she had him under the can but a foot sticking out. That sad scene unnerved her and she put a book on the can so he could not escape. She could not get herself to go near it again to release his foot and hence he stayed put for a time. A half stopped hop was his doom. But this just didn't seem right. Like the Tell-Tale Heart it inextricably called her back. So she steeled herself as best as she might and got a bit of stiff paper, lifted the can edge just enough from the floor so he could pull his foot in. Then she released the pressure just enough to slip the paper under the can and him, flip it over and scuttle him out the door.

How to Skin a Skunk

No, Mom and frogs never saw eye to eye. Placing a little frog on the tip of our finger so he could sit and grin, we would raise it up to her and say, "See how cute he is? Just look at him."

"Okay, no I don't, take it outside before it hops somewhere." She said it gave her a funny feeling in her stomach just to look at them.

Well, we just couldn't get her to fancy frogs so in the frog pens is where we kept them as well as we could.

The Deer Hunt

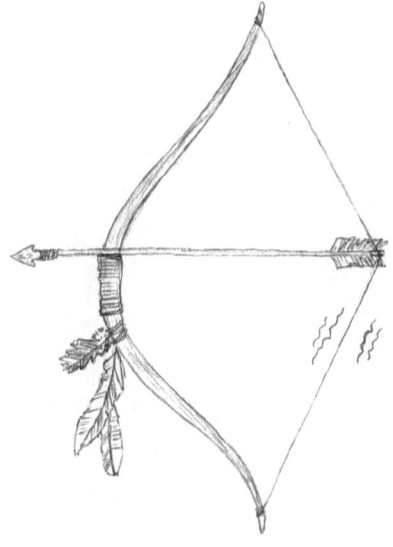

It was one of those autumn days that beckon you outside. Sunny, very cool, windless, mostly fall colors but some lingering green, and very fresh, having had a good rain a few days before. Soft earth. Ivan and I were taking advantage of this beautiful day by playing football in the small pasture just north of the house. It was a near perfect pasture for football.

Before the days of Astro Turf and manicured playing fields were the rough gridirons of early football, and ours had sported its own occasional rough spots. Gopher mounds pushed up,

How to Skin a Skunk

holes pogged in by bovine feet, and cow pies dispersed randomly about added color to our many summer football games. This time, though, it was only Ivan and me playing around. The other boys were off doing other things, and the girls couldn't be found to augment our scanty ranks. Leo and Jeremy off doing other things, though, occasioned the almost miraculous events that follow.

Rare was it that Jeremy and I were not together. But this time, little events had separated us. The day before, Leo, Andy, Jeremy and I had gone deer hunting with our bows and arrows in some hill country thirty miles from our farm. Leo had driven us there in his '66 Dodge Dart. We were unsuccessful and, having returned late, I had left my bow and arrows, my hunting knife and rope in Leo's car for the night. The bow I had used was a hand-me-down bow from Leo, his first. A long re-curve made by Bear. Its draw weight was forty pounds, comfortable enough for my skinny frame. Leo had purchased a sixty-pound short limbed Bear re-curve as his own weapon. It was nearly impossible for me to draw it to full draw, but with great effort I could, just. Once in a long while.

Ivan and I were alone because this day Leo, Andy and Jeremy decided to try a new place to hunt and left in the car, accordingly. I don't remember why I had chosen not to go, but Ivan and I were enjoying our football. As the sun reached about three o'clock in the afternoon we began to tire of it. Tossing the ball to Ivan I said, "Let's go hunting. Let's go hunting in Olsen's woods." Now Olsen's woods as we called it was about an eighty-acre patch of

The Deer Hunt

woods south of our farm. A sixty-acre pasture owned by farmer Olsen bordered our southern property line and beyond it across the county highway stood his woods.

We had explored in those woods before, and we knew the deer lived in there, as we could see them come out into the surrounding pastures to eat during the late evenings. Had even scared some up when scurrying around in there ourselves on some occasions.

The suggestion of going hunting excited Ivan as much as me, and so we hurried into the house to get our equipment. It hadn't taken but a moment of looking around when it dawned on me that all my hunting equipment had been left in Leo's car. I just couldn't believe it. "Not on such a perfect fall day as this," I thought to myself. Oh well, I wasn't going to let a bad dawn ruin the whole day. There wouldn't be much daylight left so I got really busy and scrounged about until I came up with a collection of sundry hunting articles. I laid my collection on the floor and took inventory. Here's what I ended up with:

Leo's new sixty-pound re-curve bow. Don't know why he had left it behind. Two old beat-up broadhead arrows and an old hunting knife of Leo's. The broadheads only had two cutting edges as the razors were missing. This did not add up well but you don't miss adventures because things aren't just right, so we didn't.

I was dressed in an old pair of jeans and an even older faded orange pullover sweatshirt. Ivan with not much more. It didn't feel that cold as we were still hot from our football exertions.

How to Skin a Skunk

Thus equipped, we started across the fields. Oh, and Ivan only carried his slingshot as a weapon. Anyway, we crossed our forty, ducked the fence and traversed Olsen's sixty-acre field, then across the county road into Olsen's woods.

Once we ducked into the canopy of trees we were in a world of our own. It seemed as if the whole outer world had disappeared as we entered into the forested environs. The mewing of the nuthatches and the chicka-dee-dee of Chickadees, as they flitted from tree to tree, filled the air with a cheerful and lightsome sound of the enchanted forest. The robins joined in with their territorial chirping in this late afternoon.

Everything else stood still and quiet. We began to sneak through this fairyland looking for the 'The Buck.' Now 'The Buck' is the name given to a deer that a hunter's imagination has conjured and that he feels with an almost intuitive certainty lurks about the forest. It's the one that haunts his dreams. The one that makes him say in the middle of geometry class when the teacher asks how many sides does a dodecahedron have, "Minneapolis.

Well that chimera danced around in my head as we snuck in slow motion. The mystical afternoon hosted a faint breeze chilling my skin as it crept under my tattered sweatshirt. Wistfully wishing I had put on more clothing, I crept quietly forward. I had my arrow knocked. My bow held ready.

Hooold it! I carefully motioned with my hand to Ivan (who crept behind me) to stop. There, about forty yards ahead I had spotted a doe. It was sitting, bedded down behind a log. All I could see was its head, and ears showing above it. The doe had

The Deer Hunt

not seen us. We watched motionless for awhile, but daylight was fading fast so we had to push on, knowing that when we did she would see us, and burst from her bed, running with noise and flashing her white tail through the woods, and warning every other deer of our presence.

Well, such is hunting and we continued. Sure enough, when we were about fifteen yards away she jumped from her bed and headed to our front right into the forest until we could hear her disappear in the distance. Knowing that no more deer would be right close after this commotion, we hurried another hundred yards on the soft earth and pine needle floor to take up a new position. There we found ourselves on a barely discernable farm road that snaked through the trees and bushes. We began to sneak again, noiselessly picking up our feet in slow motion and quietly placing them on the ground again. Tree squirrels from their perches on the branches scolded us in indignation for having dared enter their paradise, and the occasional chipmunk came up to get a look. Some of their expressions were so funny it almost made us laugh and disclose our presence to the deer.

Then it happened! Way up to our right and forward, where the doe's sounds of flight were last heard far off, there came a faint crashing of bushes. We stopped motionless. Was it something? Then again, a more definite crashing we heard. I turned as fast, as slowly as I could, with my finger to my lips, to Ivan behind me. "Not a sound," I indicated. But he had already frozen in rapt attention. We could both hear very distinctly the crashing of bushes. Moment by moment it grew louder.

How to Skin a Skunk

It was clear that they were deer, or something large, running at a great rate straight towards us, not caring if they made a terrible racket. The commotion hurled towards us like a freight train. We strained our ears to hear what it might be. Our eyes started from their sockets trying to pry through the brush to see what it would reveal. The approaching noise started from ahead and to our right. As it grew louder it veered to our left, still remaining out of sight. It crossed in front of us still nearer, when suddenly, above the bush tops appeared the sight of two massive sets of antlers. I couldn't see either of the deer that sported these speeding racks. One was in front of the other as they sped across in front of us about forty yards away. The antlers seemed to be only supported by the noise of popping and snapping brush and now the sound of pounding hooves. We still couldn't see the bodies. The antlers just bobbed and weaved up and down as they continued racing to the left of us.

Jumping Bejeebers! My heart was now pumping so hard it nearly leapt from my throat. Everything was happening at breakneck speed. The bucks veered again, this time almost straight towards us. This set them on a path to run by us parallel and on the left. The crashing bushes and the antlers dipping and then appearing again in rapid motion above the bushes beguiled us.

As the rush of the coming deer surged upon us, I whipped my bow up and drew the shaft and let it fly all in one motion. Almost too fast for conscious thought I had picked out an opening in the brush about eight feet wide to my left where the deer would have to dash across in their wild flight. The deer never saw us until they

The Deer Hunt

raced across that opening. I had only kept track of them by their antlers flashing above the bush tops. I intuitively let the shaft go before they reached the opening so it would meet the lead deer as it leapt across the gap. My arrow flew true with perfect timing. A loud thwack! All happened in a seamless moment: my draw, the loosed shaft, the deer bolting through the gap, the thwack, the deer disappearing into the brush, a few more crashes and silence. Not a sound. No birds, no squirrels, no breeze. We stood transfixed. A sense of unreality gripped our senses. Seconds dragged by as we stood rooted. It had all happened so fast.

As the adrenaline rush subsided, our bodies relaxed and we started whispering excitedly. "It was a BUCK! It was HUGE!" "I *got* him! Did I get him good? Sounds like I hit bone." "Should we wait to follow?" The sun was behind the horizon; just. It was getting decidedly chilly. We decided to start tracking it immediately. But where was the other buck? I had hit the first one. The antlers on the second were bigger we both agreed as we chattered excitedly. But did it go through the gap? We couldn't remember. Anyway, we hurried back the same way we had come as that was the direction the buck had run after the shot. I paralleled our previous trail going backwards. We went back and then over to a path beside ours, and sure enough there in the dust the fresh tracks of a huge deer were imprinted on a small bare crossing of dirt. A few tiny drops of blood were barely visible there also. Now I knew I hit him.

Was my aim true? The blood trail was miniscule, so down on our hands and knees we crawled, looking at every blade of grass and loose pine needle on the forest floor. Then we'd whisper, "Over here," as we spotted a drop of blood, and we'd advance a few steps further. Well it didn't seem I had got him very well. The light was fading fast. For an hour we tracked and only covered about eighty yards. This took us nearly back to where we had entered the woods. Finally, we stood up. Little hope we would find him. But standing up chanced to place me in just the right position to see him lying on the ground twenty yards ahead of us.

"There he is," I whispered to Ivan as I knocked another arrow. We snuck closer, me keeping a wary eye in case he jumped up to run again. When just ten feet away, we were really certain he was dead. Stunned at his large size and huge antlers, we gawked and stood. Slowly becoming aware of my senses, I realized I wanted to be sure there was no chance he might still be living, so I directed Ivan to shoot it with his slingshot to see if it would flinch. It didn't.

Captivated, we moved slowly and reverentially up to this Monarch of the Forest, now so quietly lying at our feet. We looked incredulously at each other and Ivan reached out and shook my hand.

But wait! How did The Buck die? There wasn't a mark on him. He lay on his side in perfect repose with no apparent wound. Where was the arrow? The wound? Marveling, we turned him over and there in his side was the tell–tale wound of a razor-less broad-head. Just a small patch of blood surrounded it. It had completely closed up, so no blood trail. But how could there be the wound with no arrow? Where was the arrow? We hadn't come across it in our trailing, so we quickly re-traced our steps

The Deer Hunt

in the hope of finding it. Still no arrow. So we backtracked from where we had picked up his trail to where I had shot at him. Nope, no arrow yet. We moved again, looking until we ended up at the exact spot where I had shot. And there in the narrow opening he rushed through when I shot, lay the arrow.

Talking excitedly, we returned to the deer.

Dressing him out was the next step in the ritual and we set to it. Well not quite. I pulled Leo's old knife from the sheath and plied it. It didn't ply. It was so dull it couldn't even begin its work. Now what to do, we wondered. Well, let's see if we can just carry the whole thing home and let Dad help with his tools from the kitchen and his butchering skill used for the cattle. We bent down and tried to lift it. With both our efforts we only managed to lift the front shoulders a fraction from the ground. We could see we were in a real bind now. It was very nearly dark. We had no choice but to summon help from home. So I stayed with my game and Ivan struck out for the house.

Forty-five minutes later and barely a glow of light left Dad arrived with sharp instruments and a rope and commenced to field dress it. He'd had to dress many a cow on our farm for meat and he made short work of this job. Having done it, he hooked a rope from one rear foot to the other and put it over his neck and lifted the hind end up to carry. I reached under the shoulders and Ivan grabbed the antlers and lifted from there. We staggered under the weight and headed for home. We went out of the woods and across the road and through Olsen's hay field, sweating and swaying with the load, when suddenly Jake appeared running in the near darkness over our pasture to help. Oh, what a welcome sight! We waited until he arrived so he could help carry it across our pasture and home. What an ordeal.

With help, I hung it in a tree, there to await Leo and Jeremy's return. They were a bit stunned when they saw what I so eagerly told them to come and look at.

It was amazing. No wonder Ivan and I couldn't lift it. After weighing it at the butchers without anything but the meat and the bones, it weighed one hundred and fifty-two pounds. Quite a large deer for our neck of the woods. Just lying there dead for Ivan and I to pick up, it would have been three hundred pounds or more. What a day. What a shot. What a deer.

But wait! What about the arrow? Upon examining the heart and the carcass the next day in good light, it was discovered that the arrow had entered the buck's side, sliced the heart, and struck the ribs on the other side, which bounced the arrow right back out the hole it had entered. Once out, the arrow fell to the ground. And there it lay, not having been carried more than a few inches from when it had hit the deer. Incredible.

Well I mounted the antlers of that huge deer. Six points on each side of the rack it sported. I cut an oval out of wood. Got a couple of beets from the garden, cut them up and boiled them until I got a rich red liquid. This I painted onto the wood as a stain and to this day that rack hangs in witness to an extraordinary adventure of my youth.

Sam

I have to wag his tale this time because the way he wags a tail doesn't translate well to paper. He's the dog, remember?

Well, this one is about his courage.

One day I trailed Jake and Jeremy along a path that ran from the edge of our property through the woodland that bordered the silica mine. Forest and bushes rose on both sides of us as we approached the more cleared land of the edge of the mine. We had just rounded the last corner as we broke into the relatively open borderland when we suddenly stopped. We were startled by two Doberman Pinschers heading right for us. Before we could even get scared (these were those same vicious Dobermans I told you about in my previous adventures), Sam smelled or saw them also.

He froze in his tracks, head up, nose twitching, staring for a moment to size up the approaching dogs. Then in a flash, his hair stood up, he growled menacingly, and then when he was sure of the situation he let himself go. We were frozen ourselves and stayed that way before the impending mayhem rattled us from our stupor.

Sam sprang forward and covered the dozen yards as if shot from a cannon. He lit into those two dogs with the most terrifying bellow we'd ever heard. He was in for the kill. He knew this was our territory and he also knew they were mean dogs and could have maimed and even killed us kids. One against two: he, a Lab-Pointer mix, not a fighting breed exactly, and they, bred for killing. And they took to it as if they meant to do it.

Never before had we seen an all out fight to the death like this. As one dog would be fighting to get Sam's throat and he theirs, teeth slammed into teeth as they clashed, white bared fangs seeming twice the normal size. The undulating screaming of sounds pierced the air. We watched as Sam drove the one back on its heels and the other jumped on him from behind and tried to grasp his rump in its powerful jaws. Sam would be drowned in squirming black and tan colors as the weight of his adversaries bore him down, and then with the roar of primordial defiance and grit he would emerge slashing and biting, twisting and turning, his white fur blurred with the brown and black of

Sam

theirs in a slurry of violent motion. The fury of it all at first stupefied us, but after that pause of stupefaction our fighting instinct kicked in and we began hollering half in horror and half with our own wounded pride. Why in the world were these beasts in our woods miles from their home and fighting our dog and ready to bite us? So we hollered, "Get him, Sam! Get him, Sam!" And we screamed and cheered him on, to bolster his courage as well as we might.

And fight he did. The caldron of fury paid no attention to landscape. The melee slammed into logs as if one. Bouncing off and tangling into the thick bushes added flying leaves to the drool from their slashing mouths. Then out onto our path and into another thicket or bouncing off another mess of downed brush they flew about. Intuitively we knew that Sam couldn't fight them to the death. Their death I mean. They would eventually kill him. So we hollered louder and more fervently trying to fill his veins with our strength too.

And it worked. He seemed in our eyes to swell to twice his size as his wrath was executed on those Dobermans. At times he seemed to be on top of both of them, and just as suddenly he would be overwhelmed and disappear under their combined assault. Our dancing around and hollering at the top of our lungs would waft him up again to the top of the fray where the fur flew and the fangs collided. And suddenly as if the decision was made instantaneously, the Dobermans broke free and streaked away as one. Sam sped in hot pursuit. And silence reigned where the instant before was a frightening din.

How to Skin a Skunk

Well, he chased them fifty yards or so until he was satisfied they were licked. He'd done his duty and came limping and whining back to us. There was blood on his ears, some minor cuts around his legs, but he didn't seem too much damaged. He was hurting though from many severe bruises and abrasions that were hidden by his fur, for he sure had fought valiantly.

He was older than those two dogs, weighed a bit less than either and, worst of all, his fangs were so worn down and blunted from all the sticks, pinecones, bones and whatnot we threw for him to retrieve (not counting all the rocks he chewed on for Jessica's sake) that he couldn't pierce his enemies' skin very well and really bite effectively, whereas these Dobermans were young, spirited, had a vicious mouthful of sharp teeth and brand new fangs.

I think if Sam were in their territory, they would have killed him. He could not have bested two of those. But because they were getting a good thrashing from him, and because they were out of their territory and in Sam's, they had had enough. It wasn't worth fighting over. That was the worst dog fight I had ever seen. Weak kneed and shaky we went back home. That kind of fury was unnerving, and we couldn't help but think what something like that directed to us would have done. Sam had protected us, with total commitment of self, in a situation where he could have lost his life for our sake.

Another instance where he threw his whole self into it was when a neighbor girl came down to visit. She was just eight or so and she brought her dog. It was a male dog, although in this

Sam

case it was a bit smaller than Sam. Don't know what kind it was, all I know is that it had brown curly hair all over.

Happened to be that at that time Leo's big sixteen foot homemade flat bottom canoe was laying on two fifty-five gallon steel drums on their side in the yard where we'd take the canoe off the car. I still have a picture of a huge bull snake I draped over the canoe when it was on those drums, but this time it wasn't about snake snits. It was about dueling dogs.

When Sam caught sight of this dog, he made no overtures of friendship to see if the trespasser was of an amiable sort. No, he lit into him with a will to do damage. This was certainly what this dog thought too. He tried to defend himself but he was completely taken off guard. He was pushed back so hard that he leapt onto the canoe bottom to escape Sam and get turned around, but Sam seemed to flow up over the canoe in a slashing of teeth and brought the war right up on and over the canoe. These two enmeshed in a tangle of teeth, fur, and each other so that they were in danger of wearing each other's skin when it was all over.

The dog parts rose over the canoe and down the other side and into the yard. We were all shouting, the little girl was screaming and general mayhem ensued. This whirlwind of fury slammed into the side of the house, knocking them both silly, giving the brown dog a chance to break free and streak for home. Sam quit chasing him just as soon as he realized he had defended his fiefdom, and he trotted back to us as if rubbing his hands in satisfaction of a job well done. Well it was, but it looked a bit un-chivalric like to traumatize a young lady so.

How to Skin a Skunk

Now to add to his protective qualities he took on air traffic too. Domestic and international was not spared. You might recall how I held off a bevy of B52's with my sling shot in the "Hear Them Roar" story"? Well Sam took this plane assignment on himself. Our forty acres was virtually a square and so it was quite a stretch to get from one side to another. Sam would chase airplanes across the whole expanse. Somehow he could see and hear jets that were flying overhead, and he would chase them all the way across the field. If they were really flying low, he would run under them as they traversed the sky over head and this would take him from one side of the property to the other. If they were way up in the blue yonder then he would run under them until he reached the edge of the property and he could go no farther. Then he would turn around and run all the way back as the plane continued over, and then turn again and run. He would do this until the plane traversed the whole heaven and disappeared. Then panting with exertion and with an exultant grin, he would return with the knowledge that he'd scared off these metal monsters that threatened us from above.

Some pilots would still risk a flight on the way to the airport by flying relatively low where we could see and hear them, but there were many more that flew so high they were only a tiny silver dot with wings, trailed by a steam cloud thirty thousand feet above the ground. With the sound trailing way behind they stayed up there the whole way across the sky. They didn't dare come down lower for fear of Sam's displeasure. He didn't except

Sam

the birds either. He would chase any bird that dared fly over, and in this way he held us in safety from any foe that may have entered from above or below.

Before I was old enough to tottle after them, Louisa, Elizabeth, and Marisa took a walk with Sam up the road. Sam usually ranged thirty feet or so in front of the group, sniffing out the good and the bad. This time he suddenly became very agitated and came rushing back to the girls. He kept himself in front of them and barked and whined. At first he allowed them to continue but he circled around them and barked. Having advanced but a short way he came and got in front of them and started to growl in a way that implied he would not let them keep going. When they realized he really meant to stop them they understood that he must have sensed some danger ahead. This made them scared, as they knew something ominous must be up there farther, and so they hurriedly turned around and hastened back to the house. The nearer they returned towards home, the more relaxed Sam became until upon reaching the house he relaxed completely.

They never knew what he was defending them from. A cougar, or a bear perhaps? It had to be more than a dog, because he accompanied us all over and dogs seldom seemed to bother him, and if they did, well you just read what he would do about it. Perhaps a person that boded no good? Seems he protected them from something that day.

It was a problem though to have him along all the time when we would go on our outdoor excursions. He was a bird dog mix

How to Skin a Skunk

so his instinct was to range about thirty yards ahead or more. Problem was he would end up scaring all the deer, squirrels, birds and any other creature we wanted to see and sneak up on. So a lot of the time he had to stay home. And oh how miserable he would look when we at the end of the property would tell him to stay home. His whole face would droop; his tail would limp, and with the most doleful look in his eyes he'd turn around and mope down the road towards home. But when we would return he would greet us with un-bounded exuberance, and then we would mollify his hurt feelings by throwing a pine cone or stick for him to retrieve.

Racing

*"These were not just chopped tops,
these were tops chopped clean off."*

—From an interview with Nathaniel B. Oakes, 11,
on the halcyon racing days of the very same;
August 20th 1971, near the "The Loop."

Chopper days, racing days. Ooohh yes, we knew about choppers. We'd seen 'em on the highway on the way to school. Motorcycles they were with handlebars that sprouted from the front like grasshopper antennas. Bikers' behinds practically dragged on the ground, forcing the rider to reach for the sky just to ride. Perhaps it was a habit they formed from meeting

How to Skin a Skunk

State Trooper issued motorcycles coming the other way. But it wasn't the motorcycle choppers we imitated. No, our toy cars and trucks mimicked the chopped cars and trucks that racing enthusiasts made from Ford trucks or Model A cars and suchlike.

Now there were two ways by which our racers became chopped. Some were by design and some were by accident. Most were a combination of both.

Mine for example was by accident. It was a Model A roadster with the top completely missing. The top was demolished in a horrific accident that happened in the fall of the previous year. Our five ton 1965 International Travelall family car had squashed my ten inch 1928 maroon roadster with a sixteen inch Michelin All Weather Steel Belted Radial Tire. In my mad rush to get to one of Rose's raspberry pies, I had recklessly abandoned my car on the driveway, and it got run over by Louisa. Still, how could Louisa have run into a parked car? How embarrassing. Fortunately no one was hurt. But my car suffered irreparable damage. The top had been ripped off. Somehow the family car showed no sign of injury and Luisa said she didn't even know she was in an accident! Anyways that's how my chopped car came into being.

Andy's car was a truck. It was about a 1965 Chevy pickup, white (well mostly rusted), its top chopped off with steel scissor like cutters from Daddy's tool box. This came about by a combination of accident and design. The accident occasioned the design. The accident was when Dad's size eleven steel toed heavy duty oil resistant leather work boot, worn in person by him, stepped on Andy's truck as it lay idling on the living room

Racing

floor. The resulting carnage was a pickup thoroughly smashed. Andy said he was thrown from the vehicle and barely escaped injury. Be that as it may, Andy got right to work, making this mangled metal truck into a racing car.

He took a big metal scissors in hand, stuck his tongue into his right cheek and chopped it off. Not his tongue. He chopped the top off. Then he switched his tongue to his left cheek and chopped off the front fenders. Don't know where his tongue tucked when he chopped the bent tailgate off to reduce drag, but there he had it. A bona fide racer. You could do that in those days. That's when toy cars and trucks were still made out of metal. The car companies hadn't wimped out yet and handed us these plastic jobbies unfortunate boys have to deal with today. One misstep nowadays from a pint sized man in soft socks is enough to reduce a boy's plastic toys to a mess of rubble.

Now if you have taken my advice from the last volume of tales and never squeezed a Honeybee, you are hearty and healthy and reading this tale and you won't have to read my description of how our driveway ended in a loop. If on the other hand you didn't read it, and you gave that little bee a firm little squeeze on his honeyed little hinder, then most deservedly you are now spluttering from your anaphylactic attack. Since you are in no shape to get down to the bookstore and get your copy (the 2 millionth copy to be sold of which you would have gotten a million dollar prize if you were the lucky one to get it) to read how our driveway ended in a loop, then pay attention really close and I'll describe it to you now. In that book I told how I took a good fast coast on a chainless bike and got topsy and turvey all mixed up out there in the pasture. Well it's the very same loop that made up our racetrack.

You see, down at the end of our driveway past the house was a loop, so you could just drive down, go around the loop and come back even with the house, facing back up the road all ready for the next trip to town. This loop was not graveled, so the surface was just pasture topsoil. Dirt, for those who live in the paved cities and have never seen any. Now, the many turns the family car took going around that loop pulverized the soil into a fine dust. By the end of the summer this dust layer laid a good inch thick at least. This it was that made the surface of our round racetrack.

Our racing machines were not powered by internal combustion gas engines measured in horse power. No, these were powered by internal combustion stomachs powered by oatmeal and Mom's bread. Engine speed was determined not by RPM's (revolutions per minute) but by BPM (beats per minute) of the oxygen starved heart.

You see, we pulled these chopped racers around the track with strings. We weren't real particular about what kind of strings. If we were fortunate we could find a whole piece of kite string. Wasn't uncommon though to have different species of string strung together to form one long one. The string from an old burlap feed sack tied to an old shoestring would work fine or perhaps a piece of old hemp rope from a hay bale. Didn't matter much. The idea was you had to hook the tyke to the truck, the kid to the car, or the boy to the bus as the case was.

Racing

We just pulled these modifieds around the track as fast as we could, the more dust boiling up the better. The most challenging thing was to keep the cars from flipping over. The track was somewhat rough, and at great speeds they would bounce, leap and lurch as we dragged them through the thick layer of dust. To help remedy this, Andy strapped a small piece of plate steel into his pickup bed, Jeremy mounted an old railroad spike under the chassis of his and I wired a chunk of steel into the undercarriage of my roadster. This kept their center of gravity really low, thus helping to prevent rollovers.

A stick from a pine tree was used to scratch a line across the track. This served both as the starting line and the finish. Typically the oldest contestant would line up near the outside of the track and the rest in descending order of age to the middle. That way the older ones were handicapped a bit as they would have a little farther to run along the outside. We had no rules about staying in lanes though. Once the race started it was every man for himself.

Now here we are all pulling up to the starting line, Andy on the outside, then Jake, next Jeremy, myself, Ivan, Peter, Tristan and last Damien. Andy says, "One, Two, Three, Go!" and we're off. We all leap forward. The dust flies from our pounding feet. Our cars all wheelie as we jerk the strings and they leap forward. The race is on.

Andy takes the lead by two car lengths, Jake in hot pursuit. I make a move to the inside to try to get ahead of the littler boys. Bad judgment. My car flips over and tumbles at the end of my string. I stop and run back to right it. I straighten up and run forward only to have to dodge around Andy's truck which has flipped. I gain a little on the little ones. Jeremy is in the lead. His car flips and now Jake leads. Andy surges forward to try to regain his position but plows into Damien who is the littlest boy way in the back and is shrouded in dust. Down he goes. Skinned knees and a bloody nose. First casualty. Jeremy's car now flips and he's running backwards to try to get to his car wreck and collides with Tristan head on. This can't be good. Tristan's down rubbing a sore arm. Second wounded. So Andy now runs ahead to catch Jake as Jeremy rights himself and his car. Andy races past me even though I'm hugging the inside with all my might. But with both lungs sucking in clouds of dust, and my heart pumping 200 BPM, my feet churning at 15 feet per second powered by Mom's high octane peanut butter and jammed bread just isn't enough to keep Andy's superior age and smarts from overtaking me. Jeremy passes me hot on Andy's tail. Jake's the one to catch and beat now but the finish line is coming on fast. Andy gains, Jeremy darts forward but there's not enough track left. Jake shoots across the finish with Andy and Jeremy seconds behind. I'm a distant fourth. Peter and Ivan never stood a chance as they tangled in the first quarter and got all tied up. The two injured little ones come sniffling up and there we all stand, gasping for air. The gasping takes on a little more urgency than under more hospitable conditions as what we gulped in was ninety percent dust. As the dust is blown away by a slight breeze we're able to get some more oxygen into our lungs. With this, the fire in our belly grows hot again. Oxygen rich, we ready for another go.

Racing

Now most of our races consisted of just one lap, but at times we opted for five. What with the normal distance being quite a lot, and the running back to right our overturned vehicles a number of times, a five lap race was quite exhausting and so, somewhat rarer.

Longer races would take some serious preparation. Racing cars are outfitted with fine tuned carburetors: only the best for high octane fuel. It was simply a matter of each one of us deciding what the best carb was for us.

Let me see, potatoes are very high carb, so is spaghetti. Beans are high carb but we all agreed should be ruled out as an unstable fuel possibly causing untimely explosion problems in the exhausting department. Yams were given a hearing but thrown out on the grounds that the name was just too wimpy. "1945 roadster pulls up to the starting line powered by yams," the announcer bellows. Nope, you can see that just wouldn't do. So it really came down to whether one stoked up on potatoes or spaghetti. Both were in great supply. Mom made nearly twenty gallons of one or the other for dinner almost every night. And as you saw already, we always topped off our tanks with a good portion of Mom's heavy high carb bread. Yep, Indy racers had nothing on us when it came to carbs.

As to the pure air required for fine tuned engines, air filters provided for this. Only the best for racing enthusiasts. Our lungs worked well for the desired effect. Pull in large draughts of dusty air and only clean air would come out on the exhale. One could easily cough up a few cups of mud after a five lap race as ample evidence of the effectiveness. Farmers' lung was a malady which inflicted farmers just as black lung did coal miners. When one used lungs as filters it tended to shorten one's breathing tenure on this earth, so we thought a pre-filter was necessitated. Thus handkerchiefs were duly brought out and (like cowboy bandits) we tied them around our mouths. These hankeys then slipped off our noses or were nearly sucked all the way into our mouths, stopping all air intake. They were abandoned accordingly. We just had to hope enough oxygen made its way past all the dust particles to keep us from asphyxiating our engines.

There were other hazards of improvised car racing. Flat tires were ubiquitous. This happened as you were trying to pass the boy in front of you and accidentally stepped on the back of his shoe. The back of the shoe would be stripped from the boys' heel and off his shoe would fly. And down he would have to sit in the middle of the track to put it back on as others swept past in a cloud of dust.

Our eyes, trying to wash the thick dust that tried to camp in the eye sockets, would get to watering so badly that the tears would mix with the sweat cascading off our foreheads and result in near blindness.

Yes, those were the racing days. The hazards only added to the fun. But you'd better get to beating all the dust off you before you come into the house or you'll be right back outside again with Mom's remonstrances echoing in your ear: "Not in here! Not in here!" Watch out! Dust off! We don't want you to miss the next adventure.

Badger Fight

One summer day in the early evening as I was playing in the dirt by the faucet at the side of the house, Leo and Andy walked by on their way to the woods. Leo had his bow and arrow and Andy carried his slingshot. Not an unusual event. Adventuring about thus accoutered was a familiar sight around the farm and I thought no more of it. Tammy arose from her place where she had been sprawled in the late afternoon sun on the gravel driveway, to follow Leo and Andy somewhat listlessly into the woods in the hope that she might be allowed to go with them. Usually, they would turn around and motion her to go home. She wasn't welcome most of the time because she would scare game away before Leo or Andy could get close to it.

I was lost in reverie as I pushed my toy trucks around in the dirt when suddenly there arose a most awful din from just inside the woods. Tammy was barking in a frantic way and the sounds were quickly turning into the sounds of mortal combat. So compelling was the urgency of her bark that I couldn't help but leap from the ground and tear up the yard onto the driveway and into the woods to see what the matter was. As I ran, I could see that Jeremy had already arrived ahead of me. Jake too, had hightailed in from somewhere to the scene. But what caught my eye was the full scale fight that was rapidly developing. I saw Leo with his knocked and drawn bow trying to get a shot at whatever was down in the bushes that I couldn't see. Andy rushed excitedly back and forth, intermittently drawing his slingshot and relaxing it as he danced about trying get a shot.

What I could see was little at first, as I was only six years old and the bushes in the woods were about my height and taller. But when I fought my way in closer, I could make out an old log that was laid over another of its fellows and a mound of dirt that had been dug from under the log. It was from behind this mound of dirt and under the log that the entire racket was coming. Tammy was barking and growling all at the same time in full out battle cry as she darted in and out at this cavern under

Badger Fight

the log. Her teeth were bared. She snapped, barked and snarled as she leapt in and darted back.

It was a frightening melee, but I just had to see so I pushed my way closer. Then I saw what all the fuss was about. A badger cornered in this hole was fiercely defending himself. He had made a most egregious mistake. He had ventured into what was Tammy territory. Well that's what she figured anyway.

Why her territory? Because if we kids played in or around something she figured it was her responsibility that we were safe. And although these woods were not technically part of our property, they bordered it. This timber was the buffer of trees that surrounded the old silica mine behind our place, and we used it as our own to play cowboys and Indians, to build tree forts and to hunt various furred and feathered critters. If we kids were involved, then Tammy saw to it that we were protected. She had wandered into the woods after Leo and Andy, caught the smell of this uninvited guest, and was intent on evicting him from the premises with all due dispatch. Only problem was, badgers don't like being summarily dispatched, due or not, them being sort of surly creatures and used to having things their own way.

Now the badger was completely cornered in this little cavern. Not a totally undesirable situation for a badger as he preferred to fight with his back up against a wall. This was so an adversary couldn't wound him from behind where he was most vulnerable. It was his front end that he was equipped to make his way into the world with. Huge claws graced his front paws used to scuttle the dirt away as he dug himself into the ground after squirrels and gophers. These same wicked claws were ample weapons against most any foe. And if this was not enough to strike fear into the unwary, his teeth were like long stout needles, made for gnashing and gashing.

Thus armed he was determined not to give way an inch. I saw him dart out at Tammy, swing his front claws in an effort to scratch her eyes out and then lunge with his head full of teeth at Tammy's tender nose. Tammy leaped back to escape these dagger thrusts and lunged at the badger as he skirted back into the burrow to shield his now exposed flank. All this while Leo and Andy tripped over bushes as they sashayed back and forth trying see the badger. The air was rent by Tammy's barks, snarling and growling, the badger in turn hissing and spitting in a most threatening manner, like a poisonous snake giving warning in its rage. An all out fight ensued.

Bedlam was unleashed, and then mayhem broke loose to see who could cause the most tumult; chaos and confusion got tangled amongst Tammy's, Leo's, and Andy's legs, just to cause more trouble. I stood transfixed as I watched the dust clouds billowing from the ground. Commotion, not to be left out, the fray entered, and there took on the sight of a most grievous fight. The badger, overwhelmed for a moment, tried to dart from his hole to escape but Tammy would have none of it. She was determined to get him. He snapped with those wicked teeth. Hissing and growling and swinging, he lunged forward. Tammy, roaring in anger, drove him back into his lair.

Elizabeth and Marisa came crashing into the bushes just as the badger hurled himself with the utmost viciousness into Tammy's

Badger Fight

face. Hit with this salvo of claws and teeth Tammy gave an inch of ground. That inch gained by his furious onslaught was just enough ground for the badger to exploit and he rushed past her. Tammy almost somersaulted over backwards trying to get him as he shot past. Turning as quickly as she might she shot in hot pursuit. The badger crashed into the bushes, Tammy following. But unfortunately she was no match for the badger. He was so much shorter he could tunnel himself through the thick brush with ease. She, being larger, had to fight through it and he quickly lost her. She trailed him with her nose, barking in frustration that she was losing him, but also warning him that he would meet with more of the same if he ever so much as set foot around our woods again.

The dust now settling along with our adrenaline, we traipsed out of the woods to re-tell the story over and over to each other in great excitement. We had never seen a badger before and oh, what a fight! Tammy eventually gave up and came back. We all gave her a lot of petting, and "Good dog!" praise as she wriggled around in our affection.

Leo and Andy eventually started out again on their adventure and I got back to my playing, but my imagination was etched with the images of a badger and dog fight so thrilling that it's just gotten into your imagination too.

Horse and Sleigh

Did anyone think to ask the horse how much he enjoyed pulling our big wooden toboggan up and down the county road? Well, I didn't either. We were having too much fun to consider it. Now the rider of the horse would invariably whoop a positive "Yippy!" Or even a "Heigh Ho!" But a horse can't ever seem to say anything but neigh, no matter on a high or a low note, and we were in no mood for a nay say.

Our friend's house fronted the county road about a quarter of a mile across the fields from us, and behind the front of the house was a very big pen, because in that pen they had a very large horse. And a very big horse is just the right size for a passel of imaginative kids. Horses left on their own on the other hand, are not very imaginative. They nicker and neigh, and perhaps nuzzle a bit when required, but mostly just munch their hay and oats, and fill the barn with fertilizer which the aforesaid passel of boys will have to clean up, like it or not.

We were all hovering around twelve at this time: Jeremy, Jake, and I, and the neighbor boys, John and Tab, and their neighbor Sean. I don't know whose brilliant idea it was to build a toboggan, I only saw and enjoyed it when it was done. Intended to be one of those sleek, light, hardwood toboggans so enviously eyed in the department stores by us youngsters and also intended to be hauled up into the hills for some coasting fun, it ended up a huge monster of a sled, uh, er toboggan. It was sort of a hybrid of the two. I'd like to call it a sloggan but then what would we do when I say I was slogging in the slush and you think I said I was slogging, not tobogganing? It would get confusing too fast, so I am going to say sled sometimes and sometimes toboggan, whichever slides the best in that part of the story.

The boys had rustled up scrap wood from the farmstead and set to with saw, hammer, and nails and ended up with a behemoth. They had nailed two 2X4 runners to one side of a piece of one-inch plywood, and then somehow curved up another big piece of plywood to make a front. It was really quite a good sled. The front curve was even closed in on the sides, so when kneeling in the front spot we could hold onto the front and our knees were hidden much like the old derby soapbox cars.

The good thing about this toboggan was that it could hold five of us at a time. The bad thing about it was that it weighed upwards of 200 pounds. Sticking to the bad for the moment, this disqualified it from mountain trips, as lugging this monster around was virtually impossible. It had somehow grown in size and weight as the project progressed.

But back to the good thing. There was a very big horse in the barn. This was a very big toboggan. And as the Philosopher says, "like likes like," and from such springs friendship. And so the horse and the toboggan were joined together that day in partnership.

They were joined together thus: A long rope was attached to the saddle and run back and attached to the front of the toboggan right in the middle. This was all done out on the county road in front of our neighbor's house. The county had plowed the road from a heavy snow fall early in the morning, so there was left on the surface of the road about four inches of slightly packed snow. To this day I don't know how the horse got enough traction to pull this sled and all of us kids, but it did. The snow was just soft enough for us not to get hurt when we fell off, but just firm enough for the horse to pull on.

Well, anyway, as soon as we had these beasts of burden attached to each other, John launched himself up into the saddle and the rest of us piled onto the sled. With a "Giddy up!" from John, the horse leaned into the rope. It seemed at first that the load would be too much for him, so two of us piled off and pushed the sled from behind to get him going. And sure enough he got going. The two jumped back onto the sled and we were off!

Horse and Sleigh

Boy, could that horse pull. Faster and faster we flew down the road as John hiegh-hoed encouragement and the sounds of our laughter filled the frosty air. We coasted thus for a couple hundred exhilarating yards until John slowed the horse and brought him to a stop and a breather. We all piled off and amidst our bantering we turned the horse and toboggan around to fly down the road in the opposite direction.

This time two stayed off to push until the horse got going and then ran and jumped on, and down the other way we merrily glided along. What exhilaration and excitement! The cold air hit us in the face and bit our noses. The clippity clop, clippity clop sang a metered song of mirth as the horse galloped powerfully down the road. Large chunks of snow thrown up from the horse's hoofs like big snowballs flew back and clobbered us on the head. Of course, it didn't take long from all trying to stay on, to everybody trying to make everybody else fall off. And this we discovered was a real hoot.

The front guy was the anchor as he could grasp the curved-up front with his hands and push his knees up under the cowling, sit back on his haunches and hang on tight. We all fought to push each other off; the front guy was the most unmovable so you had to try to grab him as others tried to push you off, or the next best thing was the guy holding onto him, and so on, until the last guy who was the most unstable. In this way one, sometimes two, and even at times all would be dragged off the toboggan. Seldom did all five stay on long. Every time one fell off he had to get up quick as he could and run to catch up and jump on the sled again. Sometimes the whole pile of us would fall off. With the lightened burden the horse would get going too fast and no one could catch up. The rider had to stop the horse until we could all pile back on the sled.

We did this a few hours a day for a week or so. That patient horse just dragged us screaming and laughing boys up and down that road without a seeming complaint. The boys took turns riding the horse. I think I would remember if I did. I don't, so I didn't. But what I do remember is the time I had being the anchor man. I wasn't the biggest or the strongest of the boys, quite the contrary, but I loved being there. I would grip as tight on the headboard as I could, and the rest would be grabbing me and pulling on me so they wouldn't be torn off by the others. With the snow flying fast from the horses hooves, and the biting wind reddening my face, the noisy exuberance of shouting and haranguing and the buffeting of everybody beating on my back and pulling on me is etched in my memory as fine as the frost was trying to etch itself onto my face. I got mighty close to heaven riding that Elijah's sliding chariot. Just as Elijah's flaming chariot, fiery steeds and singing angels filled him with joy as he raced into the gates of paradise, so I with my hot steed in cold air, and boisterous boys as my chariot companions, just missed the gates of paradise and succumbed to the old adage that on this side of heaven all must come to an end. And regrettably this too did.

It happened like this. We had been careening up and down the road for an hour or so and John had gotten off the horse and my brother Jeremy climbed up to take a turn at riding. We were once again off and running. As we raced down the road this time, I was anchorman in the front. The boys had gotten really good at holding on to each other so tightly that if one was flipped off the sloggan, he could be dragged without letting go. Of course for the boys left on, they had to grasp harder, and as anchorman, I was the last hope that the whole gang wouldn't be pulled off. As such my arms had to do a yeomen's work not to be dislodged.

With my fingers clenched over the front edge and my knees crammed under the front and my teeth clamped together, I held on with all my might. And all my might piled up and then shaken down was a mite too small I reckoned. Cuz my arms were about to come apart at the joints.

Just peel back the forty-leven layers of winter clothes I had on and you will observe that my arm did not look a whole lot different than the rope that stretched between the horse and the toboggan. But there is a joint in there which the rope did not have and it was doing some mighty complaining. Well there actually is the wrist, the elbow, and the shoulder, but we will leave the shoulder and the wrist and concentrate on the elbow. Its distress will amply illustrate my point for all three.

First, picture the yeoman mentioned before. His arm is a colossal hunk of brawn and sinew. The well sculpted muscle, the prominent veins and the manly shape. An arm fitted well for hard labor. Wait! You say you don't see that? Well my arm was doing yeoman's work, so it certainly follows that it was a yeoman's arm. You say you don't see any muscles between that lump you call an elbow and the shoulder? Well look closer! Still don't see? You must have gotten some snow in your eye. Because right...there is a muscle that is stretched so tight that it's quivering, and at the end of that muscle is a tendon, and it is hooked to the joint, and that joint is commissioned to stick together and not sunder, and to do this it's held together by ligaments. Those ligaments are so stretched they are about to break. And if they do we don't have a joint but a dis-joint, and even more a very big dis-appoint and that's the whole point!

I was holding on so tight, my arms were so taut, that they and everything else was about to fly apart, when just then the horse did a most extraordinary thing. We were approaching the driveway to the house, which left the road to the right. Just as the horse hit the entrance to the driveway, he *abruptly turned on to it at a full run.* I can see it now as plain as the day it happened.

The horse got about a half turn of his body into the drive, when as he drove his right foot down he planted solidly on a hard patch of unseen ice. His right hoof hit the ice, lost traction, and shot under him. Down the big horse went. He flipped right over. Jeremy never had a chance; the horse had turned in without warning. Flipping on the ice, he launched Jeremy right out of the saddle in a beautiful arc through the wintry sky until he landed on his behind in the deep snow in the front lawn of the horse's home. Fortunately, this was a hefty layer of snow and he got up completely unhurt. It all happened so fast! As the horse stopped, my elasticized arm contracted to normal so quickly, it practically broke. As did my sternum on the sled front as the

Horse and Sleigh

rope went slack and we stopped. The sled must have turned just enough to bring it to an abrupt stop when the horse went down cuz I don't see how we didn't just glide over him.

The horse got his hooves back under him and heaved himself back onto his feet as we all baled off the sled and ran to see if anyone was hurt. Nobody was. Jeremy had just bounced into the snow on his rump and then popped onto his feet. It did take awhile for the shot of adrenaline we got to subside. The horse ended up with some abrasions on his knee.

Well thus ended our horse sledding days. The father requested we put the horse up. Someone may well get too hurt, and the horses knee would be bruised. Well, like I said at the beginning, nobody had asked the horse what he thought of the whole matter. I guess he had just decided that he was going to turn in and he did. That's how we got turned out. But not without bringing along with us a lot of happy memories.

Cars and Kids

The first family car I remember was a 1955 Chevy station wagon that Dad had purchased five years before I was born, and the first memory I have of this car was related in the first tale I told in *The Adventures of Nathaniel B. Oakes* about playing in the tall clover on the property Dad had just bought. It was dark and we played by the light of the dome light as Dad walked the property with some of the older ones. The crickets sounded loudly and were indelibly etched in my memory. I was two.

Fast forward three years and I am five. I play in the back seat, under the seat, in the front seat, and under the front seat. At

Cars and Kids

least I remember the springs of the underside of the seats. Jeremy, Cecilia, and I were all left in the car as Dad and Mom had the little ones and were in the dealership buying a brand new light green 1965 International Travelall. It's the last memory I have of the '55 Chevy. Not a big feat as I only had two memories of it. This and the cricket night.

I can't say I have a memory of when Dad and Mom came out with the new car. My first recall was trying to climb into it after picking up Louisa, Elizabeth and Marisa from Holy Names Academy high school. How or why I was *out* of the car as we picked them up, I don't know, but I couldn't get back *into* the car. The car was way too high off the ground. You see, Dad had bought this car because of the heavy snowfalls out here on the farm. The '55 was always getting stuck. This truck had four-wheel drive and was raised up a lot higher than normal cars. Basically, a kid carrier mounted on a four-wheel drive truck frame. Sort of station wagon on a spinach diet.

So here I was on a snowy day trying to climb up onto the back-door step to get in. The only problem was my nose was not much higher than the step. I had both hands up trying to lift myself high enough to get my knee onto the step and crawl in, but I just couldn't quite do it. After I tried a couple of times, the gentle but firm hand of Louisa grabbed the seat of my britches and hoisted me up and into the car. And that's what I remember first of our new car.

And the second thing I remember was Mom being stuck with our new car in the front yard. There were two things wrong with this situation. This car was not supposed to get stuck, remember? And it didn't belong in the front yard. It was supposed to be going up the quarter mile driveway and, farther on the way, picking up the big kids from school and Dad from work. How did Mom get it unstuck? A petite five-foot-two is no match for a five-ton truck, but she somehow managed to shovel snow from under the tires and cut tree boughs from the pines along the fence line towards the mine. These branches she put under the tires, giving them traction enough to grip. So she got the truck going again. But the mystery was, how did this four-wheel drive keep getting stuck when Mom was driving it? It was a real puzzler.

Dad told us later that he finally got into the car with Mom as she was driving it to see if there was some way of discovering the answer. Settled in the seat on the passenger side, he observed. And so he discovered that it was, indeed, that she was five-foot-two and driving a five-ton truck that was the problem.

You see, with the seat pulled all the way forward toward the steering wheel for Mom, it just wasn't enough. Mom's toes were all that could reach the gas pedal. Worse, her heel was unable to rest on the floorboards. This was alright under normal driving conditions. She could just push forward enough with her toes to go. But Dad's detectering discovered that when Mom was driving in the snow and she pushed the gas pedal with her toes, the truck pulled forward too quickly and the engine would rev up too fast, thus spinning the tires and breaking them free from traction.

Since there was just enough traction to lurch the car ahead before it broke loose, it would rock the car forward and make her foot, not securely on the floor, roll back. This would make her rock forward again and her foot punch harder. Then as the car rocked, it would make her let up on the gas and then punch forward again. The pumping action on the gas pedal resulted in a constant breaking of traction. The solution was simply a big pillow placed between Mom's back and the seat. Thus, perched on the edge of the front seat, her heel now firmly on the floor, Mom was able to maneuver the Travellall around a lot better.

But another little big problem arose: Mom little, car big. Was it that in those days we didn't have push button, on the fly, four wheel drive cars or trucks? No, this problem was freezing cold hands trying to turn the hubs on the front wheel to lock the front wheels into gear. Later they improved some. They let you turn the whole hub with your hands, making it considerably easier, but in ours you had to place two fingers in one slit and your thumb in another and try to turn the hub as the wind and snow beat you around and your fingers froze and the hub refused to turn. To this day I still don't know how Mom ever did it on those stormy days. It was a challenge even for grown men. And that was not all. Inside you had to use a different stick shift to engage the transmission to make the truck four-wheel drive.

Perhaps you are at a disadvantage. You may not know what a stick shift is, much less two of them. Well give grandpa a holler while I describe how Mom used to try and wrestle the little one around trying to get it into gear. Yes, the little one. It was just out of reach enough that you had to undo the seatbelt or risk dislocating your vertebrae. A tall stickshift sprouted from the big hump that housed the transmission on the floor, and a little blighter grew about a third of that size tucked under the dash. Just of a height and far enough from the driver that to reach down there, grab the bugger, jerk it around, all the while feathering the clutch and the gas at the same time trying to get the gears to mesh and lock up was pert near impossible. I do think that a few drivers probably did go where they told their truck to go when their efforts were in vain, and the Name was too. Again I don't know how Mom ever wrestled this thing into gear.

Well it ended up being a bit of a disappointment for Dad as he intended it to be a purchase that would not only provide adequate room for all of us, but also ease the burden on Mom during the winter.

It did provide a certain entertainment for others outside the car and us little kids inside the car. But too often it proved to be an embarrassment to the teenage girls inside.

There was a gas station that we frequented for many years on the outskirts of Spokane before it was swallowed up by urban crawl. It was serviced by an elderly gentleman who loved to see our family pull up to get a refill. This was when service stations actually meant you got service.

Mom would pull up to the pump, and when she was stopped, the gentlemen would come up to the window and say, "How much?" "Filler up" was generally the reply he received, and he would commence to dispense. As the pump pumped, he would grab a squeegee and begin to wash the windows.

Cars and Kids

This is when he would start the games with us kids. Taking a big wet sponge with washer fluid on it he would find one of our little faces pushed up near the glass and splosh. He would smack it on the window right where our face was. This was before cars had tinted windows all-around. You could see right through them, well, as clear as glass. We would jerk back to avoid getting hit and then laugh ourselves silly as he went around the car sploshing and swiping our windows. He would then put his fingers right up to the glass and go all around the car pointing at each one of us as he made a great show of counting us all. He would shake his head in disbelief at all those kids and then ask Mom if this was all. It seldom was. She usually said, "No, there's more at home where these come from." Or, "No, there's some at school." We always loved it when newcomers would do the counting.

Of course, we liked him for another reason also. After counting us all and collecting the payment from Mom, he would go into the little station and come out with a handful of suckers. These were suckers with a little rope handle affixed like a loop. These he handed through the window and off we would go. Seems like a small gift now, but gas was 26 cents a gallon then, and if these suckers were a penny apiece, this was costing him a half gallon or more of gas every time we pulled up to the pump. Well, the tentacles of the town crept ever closer and choked out this little fuel outpost, but I will always remember him as a kindly old gentleman and he deserves to be immortalized in these pages. And now he is.

How to Skin a Skunk

The counting business did not stop there. No, she and we got this question many times. Truck drivers sitting a mile high above us in their big semi's would look down at us when they would be parked alongside at a stoplight and make a great show of counting us all. When done they would shake their heads and laugh. Of course, the big sisters would shrink down and try to disappear under the car seats but we little boys would be pumping our arms up and down in the sign that all little boys know, trying to get the trucker to blow his air horn. So, with a shake of their heads they would reach up to the top of their cabs and let blow a huge blast on the horn as they drove away.

Our big ole Travelall took us on family adventures too. Fun trips. Dad would take us for a Sunday drive. Mom would pack up a parcel for lunches and in we would pile. I don't know if Dad really had any particular end in mind as he would travel out of town. He would choose a highway that headed out. Could be towards Idaho and sometimes beyond. Even a little into Montana or perhaps south into the Palouse Country of miles of rolling grain fields. Or north up to the mountains towards Canada. West would take one into the sagebrush country, wide open cattle country.

One memorable trip was the time we went into Montana. The Travelall, being four-wheel drive, and me just seven or so, it always seemed we were up pretty high. And we seemed to be a lot higher up when Dad was crossing a remote mountain pass somewhere in Montana. The road was little more than a jackrabbit trail winding up the mountain. You object that jackrabbits don't live in the mountains. You'd be right. I said it was very little used. A few bi-annual trips of the plains jackrabbit to their relatives the snowshoes in the mountains and you can see that this was a very primitive road.

We all wanted to see outside to the scenery. There were no seatbelts in those days except, perhaps for the driver, so we could all pile by the windows. As I looked down from where I was, I was looking straight down the mountain side because Dad was so close to the edge you couldn't see the shoulder of the road. I thought we were going to fall straight down. It was a veritable cliff on the right side going up. And we were going up. Straight to heaven in more ways than one if Dad wasn't very careful. At times I think it was the butterflies in our stomachs that kept the car lifted up so it couldn't fall over the side.

We made it though. And the next thing I remember we were exploring an old abandoned boat on a huge river I don't know where. Maybe you do. I can't find it on the maps. Perhaps they don't know where it is either. Anyway, someone had abandoned a good size steel hulled boat. Somewhere around twenty feet long I suppose. After Dad had pushed up against it hard and made sure it couldn't shift around, he allowed us to crawl up and onto the deck. It was leaned over as if a little tired and sat with its hull somewhat still in the water. Dad lifted a huge steel hatch so we could peer down into the depths. A steel ladder tempted the older ones to go down inside. So Dad went first and the older ones followed. Lastly I went down. It was scary. It was so dark and we didn't have a flashlight. Our voices echoed off the steel sides as we walked and looked around in the feeble light. The musty rusty smell enveloped us all and gave us kind of a creepy feeling. We groped around in there and some hollered to make an echo.

So intent was I on all this suspense that I didn't notice what was once only a creepy emotional feeling was quickly turning into a very this worldly feeling right down to my toes. Creeping surreptitiously through the stitches of my shoes was icy water. I don't remember what exclamation I made, at seven my repertoire was quite small, but it got the immediate attention of one of the big kids and I was yanked up off the floor and onto the ladder. There I was commandeered up the ladder and spit out of the hatch onto the deck. The others quickly scaled the ladder and spilled onto the deck with varying degrees of soaked socks. We all got back to the car and pulled our shoes off and then the socks. Doing it the other way around creates quite a challenge.

Can't do a lot to help soaked shoes, but we wrung the soaked socks until they looked very limpy and got them put back on to our feet. Then we had to put on our very cold shoes. We were kind of miserable going back over the mountain pass until the car heater was able to get us toasty warm again.

Seven years later that Travelall couldn't travel with all, less or few. No, one day Dad was driving Elizabeth to work and as he entered an intersection on a green light, a fellow was whistling a love song, I imagine, that went something like this; "Roses are red, Violets are blue, the light is red, come on through." And so,

Cars and Kids

he did. Fast. T-boned the car right at Elizabeth's door. Threw our big car around and onto the curb. Elizabeth got a broken pelvis. Dad was banged up, and our big greenish kid cart was no more. Bent irretrievably in half.

So the responsibility of toting toddlers and teenagers was seated in a 1967 Chevy Carryall. It was the precursor to the more modern Chevy Suburban. It had a bench seat in the front, was an automatic, and was only a two wheel drive. It had a three quarter seat behind the driver. It only had one back side door on the passenger side which left a space to go back to another full seat. Behind that was a cargo space where any extraneous children were deposited. Sardines enjoyed a bit more comfort in their tins than we sometimes had, but overall it was a good carryall.

Now it was at some times embarrassing to be stopped at a light and have people express surprise at our huge number of kids and start counting (they looked in just as if we were fish in a bowl). We couldn't try to pass off the tale that we weren't all related, just a bunch of friends together, as the stamp of Oakes was clearly demarked on all of our features. Shakespeare says that "the world is a stage and we all act our part on it." Well our stage was a big red car and we could all be seen acting in it.

Imagine the day we had to endure the humiliation of the front wheel shock absorbers failing, both at the same time! They're meant to suppress or cushion the action of the springs as they bend and unbend so a vehicle doesn't bounce up and down all over the road when traversing bumps. Lose those shocks and watch out. We did watch, in horror, as everybody else watched too.

How to Skin a Skunk

Mom would accelerate from the stopped position and the whole front of the car would lift into the air as the springs stretched unencumbered from the shocks to their full height. The car looked just like an ocean liner when a big wave lifts the front of the ship until the whole thing slants way up. Then when Mom eased off the gas (having reached the desired speed), the car would nosedive back towards the street as the springs compressed all the way. Now the nose of the car would be inches from the ground, the whole car slanted ridiculously forward. Driving down the road further, now the nose would go back up, and then down as the springs took full advantage of their liberty.

So here we were speeding ahead with the car rising and falling as if on a huge undulating wave. If it was far to the next stop, the waving would start evening out and the car moved in a more dignified fashion. But the humiliation was not to end. As soon as Mom began to slow down, the nose would dive to nuzzle the pavement again, and then pop up to look for the stars, with all our heads bobbing up and down to the rhythm. It got worse as she braked harder for the stop. Well at last the stop would come.

Alas! All the forward momentum was transferred to the unfettered springs, and as we remained stopped at the light, there we would be, the front of the car bouncing up and down and us looking like bobble-heads to all the startled drivers around us. We feigned the most nonchalant attitude we could muster. Like a disobedient horse, the car would rear up and come down as if charging at the bit to get going on another rearing and bucking ride down the highway and so it went.

Cars and Kids

Mom would accelerate and off we would go to entertain the startled masses with another rodeo ride down the street as we tried to hide the red in our faces.

I think the residual effect of the shame still played upon our features when we arrived at the house to tell Dad about our adventure. When we had to brave this charade again the next day on the way to school, Dad driving to pick up new shocks at the parts store, we could see an inkling of cracks appearing in his stoicism. A half smile played around his lips and his eyes laughed as he saw our discombobulation and tried to ignore the entertainment that was so pleasing to the audience that beheld our cavorting car.

The Cows Are Out!

I like cows. Always have. I like the cute little calves with their over-sized ears, big round eyes and puggie little noses. I like the big masculine bull, the fattening steers and the placid milk cows. I can even stomach them well when introduced as steak, roast or hamburger. They are my favorite barnyard animal. But *in* the barnyard, not *out*.

That was the problem though. They preferred out, not in.

"You have to get up, boys," Mom would say as she shook us out of our beds at five in the morning. "The cows are out and in Bomsted's field." "Get up, honey," as she would shake Rose and the other girls from their slumbers. Each one of us kids would be shaken from our pleasant dreams. "Oh no, not again," we would murmur through the haze of fast retreating sleep. "Bomsted's? Way across in Bomsted's?" Now Bomsted's place was clean across our forty-acre field and into the next forty and that was no place we wanted to be at that hour.

So up we would get all muttering and murmuring as to who might have left the gate open, did they break the wire or not, were they going to get bloated by eating in a different field, and such like questions. Couldn't tell such things of course until we got out there to see for ourselves. And who wanted to go out into the rain and sleet? But up we would get, and begrudgingly get into our work clothes.

It wasn't supposed to be like that. We were supposed to repose in quiet slumber until the time to get up for school in another half an hour. Then eat four pounds of hot oatmeal, sugar and milk, and three pounds of Mom's bread thickly layered with butter and jam, all the while darting to the newly lit wood stove to take the chill out of our early morning bones. Then don our chore clothes and do the chores before coming in and getting all set up for school.

Well, anyway, outside, hungry, sleepy, and with cold bones we dragged ourselves across the field, a whole quarter of a mile across our field and then into Bomsted's pasture. Sure enough, there was our whole herd, all hurriedly, guiltily, tying their tongues around the biggest chunks of stolen fodder they could get. Ripping it from the roots and gulping it down and acting like they didn't see us coming. And then, as if on cue, they all raised their heads and looked wide eyed at us with a big blank stare, as if to say, "What? What are you looking at?"

They darned well knew what we were looking at, and we began to encircle them to push them back into our field, and they of course wanted more of that contraband, and so turned and ran. Well, we were too smart for them and kept them from getting further into Bomsted's field, but when pushed back toward our fence the fun began.

At that time there were only sections of the property that were fenced with either barbed wire or sheep wire. The rest and still the majority were fenced with one strand of electric wire. Under normal conditions this is a very economical and sufficient means of keeping cows in the pasture. It is used extensively across this good old U.S.A. But on our farm the bovine brain was not normal. In normal circumstances cows hate to get shocked by electric fences as much as farm kids do. Abnormal conditions would sometimes force them to overcome their fear of the fence. Such conditions as biting horseflies, much greener fields on the other side, or anything that excited the other passions more than the fear of the fence. Much the same as the boy running from a mad rooster or angry wasp would run through the electric without a howdy doo. But it didn't take any such abnormalities for our cows to wander.

Now, you couldn't actually ask them why they wanted out rather than in. You just had to draw conclusions from where you found them.

The Cows Are Out!

Like the time Mrs. Hall came down the driveway to inform us that our cows were out and in her field. How did she know? Well, when she stepped into her living room there were a herd of cows looking in her window. When you're a twelve hundred pound beast it's hard to hide behind clumps of pasture grass or the skirts of ladybugs. She didn't have any difficulty identifying them as our cows.

Or the time our steers Tom and Jerry followed their mother June through our woods, caddie corner through the old mine, across Johnson's wood lot, and then beyond to the top of the Big Hill where you could see for miles around. A goodly mile from home. They might have been out there still enjoying the sights today if they hadn't left their muddy footprints in the newly wet snow.

Well why in the world were they in Bomsted's field on a wet and windy morning? Our pasture was as good as theirs. I don't know, but maybe it just fits that mysterious falsehood that all sin carries. To wit, if a good is ill gotten there is more pleasure in it. They were sure enjoying chomping down on stolen property. And whatever reason they had, we had to get them out of there and back home.

As it turned out, they had broken through the wire this time, and fortunately for us it had snapped at the place they pushed at. Many times it would snap hundreds of feet away. Since it had snapped there, all we had to do was push them back through the gap the broken wire left. Sounds easy. Only problem is, cows remember where the fence ought to be and are mortally afraid to cross the ground where they know it ought to be. Now why do they get the courage to break through a live wire and then become all wobbly like when asked to go back through a hole in the fence? They seem more afraid to cross the fence line when there is no fence than when there is.

So here we are trying to make the cows go back through the fence to our side of the pasture. We tighten the noose. They approach the break. Then one brave cow stands a few feet back from where she knows the fence should be and stretches her neck way out and sniffs up and down trying to locate the wire. The others come crowding up and watch in intense concentration. For no known reason the stretched cow whips around to run as if she had been shocked. We lunge toward the place she hopes to escape and close her off. We tighten the noose more.

Another cow stretches out to do the same thing. This is where you have to have everybody stop and stay perfectly still to let the cow figure it out. The cow stretches even more. Takes a tentative step forward.

Funny to see the cow body leaning back so as to sprint backwards, but at the same time her head still fully extended as she moves slowly forward. Half her body gets across before she realizes she is already past the fence line, so she bolts forward as if shot from a cannon. That's all it takes for the others to shoot the gap and into our field. Nothing left for us but to repair the wire and troop back to breakfast, having been routed out of bed by bad bovines.

One time they were found in the pet cemetery a neighbor had set up. There he planted pets. I don't know why, as wheat

The Cows Are Out!

and alfalfa were the preferred crops in our part of the country. Perhaps it was a new way to raise pets.

Anyway, the cemetery had nice grass and we found our cows there harvesting it with gastronomic delight. It wasn't hard to herd them out of it this time though. The looks on our faces for having found them there let them know with little uncertainty that we would gladly make them permanent residents amongst those attractive stone monuments.

There were many other times we found them in forbidden pastures and threatened with turning them into hamburgers. Then they would really wish that hamburgers were porcine (and not bovine) as the name implies.

Well, if you're getting a little tired as I am, what with getting out of bed at these early hours to chase cows, I'll end this tale, get some sleep and join you on the next adventure. But not a cow tail tale this time.

Noses and Toeses

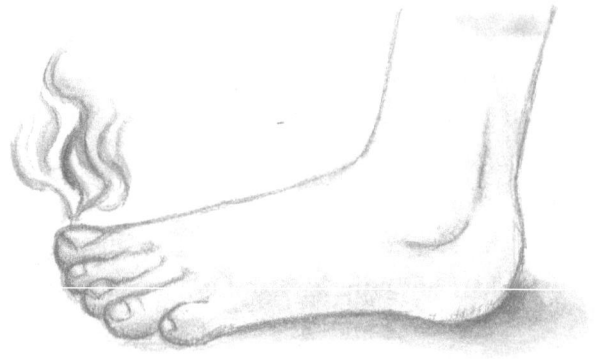

How many times have your toes actually met your nose? Really met them. Up close and personal. I mean you wouldn't expect them to be the closest relatives. I know they are connected to the same trunk, but there is quite a stretch of humanity between them. Have they really shook hands or are they content to let themselves mind their own business as in letting the nose do the smelling from up there in rarefied air and the toes down there in the dirt do the walking? They do cooperate of course for the common good of the body, as all parts ought to in a well ordered whole. Here the one odiferates and the other ambulates.

Thus smelling is a good example of shared interest. The nose smells as its principal function. It pleases us by alerting us to

Noses and Toeses

pleasant perfumes, delicious foods, perhaps warning us off of putrefied pottage. The feet, on the other hand, have as their principal function to walk, but under the right circumstances they become real good smellers. The rottener they become the riper they smell. By Uncle Sam! I could sometimes smell Jeremy's feet from across the house after him shucking his shoes and snapping his socks off. Especially after a day of tramping the field, wading creeks and chasing cows.

Parenthetically, If you hadn't actually seen him shedding his socks and just caught the fumes permeating the house, then perhaps you might think at first that Tristan was trying to cook week old lizard lips or Damien bringing in an old gopher that should have been R.I.P.'ed a week ago under the ground but had instead ripened atop the soil under the sun.

Anyway, however you put it, noses and toeses should only have fleeting visits for the health of the body, but a number of times noses and toeses did tragically meet before a proper introduction may have averted disaster. I know because it was my nose and my toes.

One night, on account of the overflow of kids, I was sleeping on the floor next to the living room couch and Peter was sleeping on the couch. So far so good, sleeping is a relatively safe pastime. Nobody gets hurt. And all are happy in dreamland. Until....

Up pops Peter. Something to do with his piping. It was pitch dark in the house. That's okay, we were all used to that and we could all maneuver quite well in the blackness on our way to the bathroom. Peter swings his feet off the sofa and onto my chest. He stands. Slipping on that mountain which stuck up like the breast bone of a starved chicken, he begins to fall. He takes a quick step with his right foot to catch his balance and steps solidly on my face. Realizing he is not on the floor but on my face he tries to thrust himself off while still trying to stand. His big toenail bites into the side of my nose, trying to get a grip as he is falling.

Now from the bottom of my beak to the top of its peak is not quite the Matterhorn, but it is a somewhat prominent protrusion and Peter found it quite so in his predicament. He tried desperately to climb over it to the floor beyond. I, in the meantime, was trying to coax some air into my squished rib cage through my snout, the most natural appendage to get air through but which was now being mauled by Peter's feet as he tried to climb this midnight Mountain. His big toe having got a grip, slipped, and as a consequence his toenail scraped down the side of my nose, leaving a gash such as an avalanche makes as it sloughs off the mountain side. He was able to extricate his left foot from my crushed chest and step onto the floor just as his right cleaned the peak off my nose as it flew past.

So after all this kerfuffel (a kerffuffle is not a muffled curse, although it might be mistaken as one), sleep was slain and I assayed the damage by passing a hand over my trod upon face. Where nose and toes had met, a wound left a stream of blood flowing down my nose and beyond. Peter and I rushed as well as we could in the dark to the bathroom whereupon, flipping on the light, I beheld where the wound was.

Noses and Toeses

Now if only Peter Piper had picked a peck of Pied Pipers instead of a peck of pickled peppers perhaps The Pied Piper that Peter was piped by into the darkness would not have been around to play his pipping pipe, and my nose and his toes would have remained only distant acquaintances.

Alas I could only have hoped. As I attended school for the next few days there were many questions, All sounding like this: WHAT HAPPENED TO YOUR NOSE?? I couldn't lie. My nose couldn't have stood anymore stretching. I just had to tell them that my little brother had stood on it, and then disappear in embarrassment as rapidly as I could, so the follow up questions could not be asked. To this day there is a very light white scar that skids down the side of my nose like the mark of an ancient avalanche. Most, I would assume, conclude upon seeing it that it is one of many battle scars from my youth, battling bad guys, slaying dragons, anything to rescue damsels in distress, but no, now you know as I know, it was just an unfortunate meeting of my nose with his toes.

One time it was my nose and my toes. I was quite little and we thought it would be great fun to jump off the top of the cab of the 1936 one ton truck. So we crawled up the front bumper, up the fenders, onto the bonnet, over the windshield and onto the top of the cab. Seemed we could see for miles being up so high.

Looked like delicious fun to fly all the way down. Might even be in the air a whole half of a second. Not bad for a boy who is not a bird and not meant to fly at all.

How to Skin a Skunk

So I jumped and indeed that half of a second went awfully fast and when I hit the ground my nose hit my toes. My legs just did not have the strength to absorb the shock of hitting the ground. The ligaments that masqueraded as muscles just weren't up to the task and so my legs bent at the knees and the hips, my back collapsed forward and my nose met my toes. It wasn't a happy meeting. In fact it made me cry. I was determined from that time on that noses and toeses were to remain in their respective far apart spheres without too close of a friendship. Until Peter, but I already told you about that.

Animal House

Have you ever had this phrase hurled at you when you've left the door open upon entering a house? "What's the matter? Were ya raised in a barn?" Well some of us were, and I could answer that by saying, "Yes." Well no, not in a barn, but the house was utilized as one quite a number of times when necessity called.

Over the years we swilled swine, coddled calves, thawed thumpers, patted porcupines, snuck snakes, teased toads, and arrested thieving magpies in there.

How to Skin a Skunk

But it's the farm animals that I want to talk about. These were invited in on account of their health, not on account of entertainment. And their invitation was not unconditional.

The time the baby pigs were brought in was one of those times.

Now there is an experience very common on farms, namely that the farmer's plan as to when a farm animal ought to give birth differs from when the animal thinks it is time. For the farmer, a sunny, warm midmorning after chores, after breakfast, no wind and only balmy weather ahead for at least a week fits his humor just fine.

For the animal, just after that balmy week. For a horse to foal, it must be foul. For goats, are you kidding? It has to be after dark, before supper, a cold brisk wind blowing. Pigs? The one year after the Middle Ages that happens to have a late snow in early summer, that's their time.

Cows? After midnight, rain at minimum, a little hail and wind to freeze the farmer usually, and especially if mamma cow is having a very difficult time. You get the picture. Everything must be opposite from the farmer's comfort.

And so it was this night with the pigs. Dad had built a farrowing shed wherein the sow was to have its piglets. A small shed, just big enough in length to accommodate a large sow laying down and wide enough to allow room for the piglets to roam away after birth. Where she lays down, fences on both sides allow the piglets to get under a strategically placed heat lamp; but mostly allow them to escape her. Mama pigs are notorious for not checking well when they lie down, and they often squish their little ones before the littles can get out of the way. Hence

Animal House

the double fence. While the shed was fine for swine, it was not for tots. It wasn't big enough to fit us in also.

As the sow would deliver each piglet, we had to grab it, clean it, and place it under the heat lamp or get it to nurse. Problem was, sometimes the sow has all the little ones lickety-split, one right after another, a right efficient quick work. Other times the piglets mosey on out, and there can be considerable time between when these little squirts enter the world. Many a sow can have up to twelve babies, and even when paying attention and acting smart, the piglets get out into the world in a couple of hours. But if they are lollygagging and just waltzing out, they can take up to eight hours or more.

And so it was in this case. We froze our noses and toeses and everything in between waiting for these little piggies to dance into the world. You see, as I mentioned, there wasn't room for us to sit in the shed. We had to sit out under the sky.

The first one came when it started to rain, the next when hailing. In case we got a little warm by snuggling into our winter wraps aided by an additional blanket, the wind would gust up and breach the rampart of wraps and send in the chill. So there we sat shivering and shaking waiting for the next installment, and suddenly one would appear. Then it was all business and excitement: Cleaning it, warming it, and getting it to eat.

This lasted from about 7:00 pm to 5:00 am when we finally gave up on expecting another.

Thoroughly frozen, hunger pangs added to frozen limbs, we all headed to the house.

This panoply of piglets occurred during a very late and cold weather pattern. Normally a heat lamp would be sufficient to keep the piglets warm in the shed. But a few hours later, after we had gone to bed for some much needed rest, Andy noticed, as he fed the rest of the pigs, that the little ones were still too cold in the shed and they might be lost to a chill.

Suggestions were passed around. What to do? Depending on the age, sex, and status of the kid, various answers were forthcoming. Such as…

Damien, four-year-old male: "They can sleep with me!" He could just imagine how fun it would be to have all these small pink curly tailed porkers running around in the bed to play with. Mom said pigs-in-a-blanket is a fine metaphor for pork meals but is not to be taken literally. So no. Decidedly not.

Rose, fourteen, the frozen rabbit girl whom I will tell you about in a moment, emphatically stated, "There will be no pigs anywhere near my bed. Hotdogs are fine, even with relish, but not when they are still on the hoof."

Andy suggested we build a pen in the living room. But a hog farm in the middle of the family room was not to Mom's liking.

So it was decided by Dad that the best solution was to use for a pen the big oblong galvanized tub that we had used as our first bathtub years before. Jake and Jeremy went out to get that and put sawdust in the bottom of it. The rest of us went up to the pigpens to catch the piglets to put them in the tub. Easier said than done. When little pigs are chased, they squeal: really, really loudly! And when they are caught? They squeal as if there is no tomorrow.

Animal House

Two of us got into the shed, one each, on opposite sides of the sow, behind the barriers where the heat lamps were. Down on our knees in a cramped space, we tried to grab these piggies as they squirted around the floor, screaming, squealing and crying bloody murder. The enraged sow tried to turn around and break into our spaces to get at us, at the same time squealing her own frustration and concern for her babies. She must have thought we were making live sausages right there. What a melee of pandemonium stacked on chaos that was! Ear splitting complaints assailed us as we caught and placed each one into the tub. Finally, the last one was caught and released into confinement. The cacophony subsided to worried grunts from the sow. We lugged that tub full of prandial pigs down to the house and into the living room and set it in front of the wood stove.

They didn't get much rest at first. Piglets are awfully cute, and we watched them darting around, kicking up their heels and having a great time in the warmth of the house. Their welcome, though, only lasted the rest of that day and the night following. They had to be taken out and let nurse a few times, with the predictable mayhem that followed in getting them back into the tub.

All in all, it's better to keep the pig in the poke than in your house. So they were turned back over to the sow when the dangerous cold had passed.

But what is this about Rose and the frozen bunny? Well it was Rosie's chore to take care of the rabbits. She did so assiduously and they multiplied exponentially, as rabbits will. One morning was a near disaster when the weather tried to blunt this prolific increase. There were six or seven bunnies in this particular batch, all matured just enough to have all their fur, and their eyes open. They could barely get up and hop about. They were still quite small. Just a hair (no not a hare, these were rabbits), but just a hair bigger than the palm of your hand. We used empty tuna cans as food and water dishes. These Dad wired to the side of the cages so they couldn't be knocked over.

One cold morning Rose went out to feed and water the rabbits. When to her astonishment she saw there was a bunny frozen in the water can. Here he was, completely alive, his whole back end enveloped in solid ice. How he ended up in the water in the first place we could never figure, but there he was stuck fast.

Rose rushed into the house with the can in her hand and the bunny poking out.

To get out his frozen-in fanny, Mom turned the oven on and opened the oven door. There on the door Rose set him. The heat of the oven slowly thawed the ice, and after a bit the bunny was extricated. Rose buffed him up with a dish towel to get his circulation going and soon the bunny was contentedly hopping about. It would have taken a long time to freeze that water as he sat in it and why he didn't die is a mystery. But we had great fun roasting bunny buns that morning.

Now I had mentioned that Andy suggested we build a pen for the piglets when they needed to come into the house. It ended up we did have to make a pen there in any case.

Animal House

One of our cows had decided that froze in the snows was better than fun in the sun and dropped her calf into a snow bank. Made a soft landing, I'm sure the calf thought. But what about my circulation, he wondered. We didn't think ice in her veins was such a good idea either, so we took the calf into the house. Where else? There was heat emanating happily out of the sides of the big fifty-five gallon drum wood stove, ready to limber up the cold and stiff who sought a thaw.

So the kitchen chairs were arrayed in a circle with their backs turned towards each other and sides touching. Then we roped them together with baling twine. It made a right tidy pen for the calf. So again, with warm towels the calf was all massaged and buffed up until his blood was merrily flowing through his veins.

We then stuck him in his makeshift pen, until he stood up and started looking for something to eat. We had to take him out to nurse a few times to get the cow to accept him and to get his meals. But we just couldn't leave him out there because it was far too cold. So there we had a calf living in the living room for a couple of days. But he too had to return to his own habitat with his bovine buddies.

Jake found the porcupine. We would see and chase porcupines at times. We even had to pull their quills out of our dogs' mouths when they got too up close and personal to these spikies. But this was different. Jake found a baby one. It was barely bigger than his fist. It was cuter than a bug's ear. Look at a bug's ear to see if you agree. Jake brought it into the house to show us all. He had to wear thick cotton gloves that Dad would wear at work. Even though this 'pine was just a little critter, he still had quite an arsenal of quills. After oohing and aahing and some of us putting on gloves to hold him, it was decided we could not keep him. It is true he was very friendly. But it was agreed that he would make a very prickly bedfellow and a quick glance at all the wooden furniture that looked pretty knawable convinced us that his being inside might turn us outside, so Jake had to take him back to where he found him. Which takes us from porcine to porcupine with a bunny and bovine in between.

We snuck snakes in but we were never able to keep them in the house. Mom's experience with our frogs convinced her we would never be able to keep them in their pens. So to sneak a snake in to snuggle would have gotten us into big trouble.

Trouble, yes. Jeremy brought our snake snatching to college where the frog race ran. He brought a good sized bull snake into his dorm room and put it into a nice tight aquarium. Or so he thought. After theology class (discussing the Fall of Man and the Serpent, no doubt), he came into his room and made his way to the snake. What!? It was gone. How could that be? Better yet, where could it be? The second question seemed a little more urgent to answer. A thorough search of the room and a check to make sure no one had taken it for a walk turned out to be fruitless. Jeremy began dismantling the coverings of the bed. And there, as if swinging in a hammock, was the snake. You couldn't see him through the sheet but he had crawled under

Animal House

it. Where the sheet was tucked into the side of the bed, he had crawled the length and sagged down over the bed frame. Jeremy stripped the bed and extricated the snake. Kind of made us glad we kept the baby rattlesnake in its glass jar down by the creek!

Pig Slop

To slop a pig is to feed pig slop. And when you slop the pig his slop he will slop it all up. And pigs do slop. They slop a lot. Slurp to be sure. But their slurping is just plain mild compared to their slopping.

And so we come to Andy. It can be a little confusing this slopping business. Sometimes he slopped through the mud with slop to feed the pigs their slop. And the pig then slopped his slop while standing in slop. So with Andy slopping the slop and the

Pig Slop

pig slopping his slop while both stood in slop makes this tale very sloppy. Trouble is: if we stop the slop the pig will get hungry.

But enough of this. Andy was not allowed to stop and so he continues to slop. But the tale stops slopping.

Alongside the wooden pen where we kept the sows and piglets we had a very heavy duty pig pen. This is where we kept the boar. Although they are named boars, they are not boring. They aren't invited to parties just as other boors aren't, but not because of a lack of personality, but rather because of just too much. They can get very aggressive. And we would get a quick look like this: Leo would grab some of us littler boys and swing us up and almost over the pen wall to scare the bejeebers out of us. No kid is any good without his bejeebers in him. Even grownups have a hard time without them and use wine or whiskey to bolster them up when bejeeberless, but usually this just results in blubbering. Better to hold fast to your bejeebers.

A big male pig sports some pretty mean tusks, and along with them a pretty mean temper, so we were not allowed in his pen. Clem was our boar's name. He wasn't a huge boar. Fair to middling in size, but he could be very distempered. Consequently, only the older boys were allowed into his pen when necessary. Dad had turned 3'x3' concrete pipes on their ends while butting their sides together. This made for a veritable concrete wall. It was shaped in a rectangle. We tried to use the turned up pipe for frog pens but frogs could climb up the rough concrete sides and get out. We did keep some nice big gopher snakes in them at times though!

How to Skin a Skunk

Andy was good at coming up with little ditties or rhymes as he made his rounds slopping the pigs. I'll write one down, but I'm a little puzzled. I don't know if he thought it or not. If he did think it, I inked it. If he didn't think it, I didn't ink it. How could I ink what he didn't think? But I did ink it. Here it is. But did I think it? Not that I thought. Well, anyways, it is inked. Read it. If Andy says he didn't think it, I at least know I inked it. So I might have thinked it.

Anyhow, I don't claim it's good. But it helps getting you through the slopping of swine. So if you need a little help when your swine are swilling, feel free to use this ditty or better yet come up with something sweller. It's even better if you can get your pigs to jig, but I think that would take a wigglier poetry than mine.

>I carried the slop in a pan or pot,
>on a walk or a run, but not a fast trot.
>I carried it to the pens
>Where the pigs were kept in,
>In a hurry to feed them their din(ner).
>There I commenced
>to jump over the fence
>and so into the sty I flew:
>But in utter dismay
>I was stuck there to stay
>as into the muck I did plop.
>Yew yuck, what dirty luck,

Pig Slop

To be stuck here in the sty.
Was I to dine
with the swine
this time?
I would not
if I could not
so I didn't.
Why?
Well, have you ever dined
with swine
While held fast in filthy brine?
Well, if you haven't,
you mustn't,
It makes the pig unplusunt,
your supper a bit supine,
so I dropped the slop
and grabbed a Knot
tied into a rope, in my pocket.
I needed a noose
to get myself loose, so...
With double over ought
and underbelly shot,
I quickly formed a loop.
This I hied over the gatepost top
and pulled with all my might.
I heaved and I hoved
and I got my cramped toes

How to Skin a Skunk

>outa my budgeless boots.
>I swung a'swooshing
>and over the fence I plopped.
>I glared at my soiled socks
>and muttered in disgust,
>>"To be stuck in the sty is nothing but stupid,
>>but is better than a stick in the eye."

I never did see Andy's name in the *Best of Porcine Poetry* must reads, but his hamming it up humored us throughout the years. Of course the hog slopping years faded away with time when Andy grew up, but the swine swilled kept us filled. Oh no! Another silly poem I feel is on the way. Get into the next tale quickly!

Big Boots to Fill

One year, we had a very unusual winter. I was quite little, four or five tops. It was the year a lake formed in our forty acres, about three hundred yards from the house to the south. Our land was relatively flat, although the eastern part was a little higher than the northwest where our house stood. A small swale ran from the north to the south, and near the southern fence line there was a four acre area which would be slightly wet and stay quite green until late in the summer.

How to Skin a Skunk

Somehow the confluence of snow, freezing rain and so on, left seven or eight inches of snow on the ground and a big lake in the four acre area. If I remember correctly the lake was about five inches deep and was on top of the snow. I can only guess that the ground had frozen. Snow then came. It thawed enough to melt some which began to flow down hill beneath the top snow to collect in the swale. Must have frozen again over that and then snowed again. Howsoever it miraculously came about, we awoke one morning to behold a beautiful lake in the field.

We seldom saw geese in those days. Some V formations would fly high overhead during the migration seasons but that was a rare treat.

This year was different. A gaggle of geese came and landed on the lake: Lots of gooses and ganders but no giggles.

Now the funny thing is I don't know where I am going with this story because I don't remember why I was going with Dad that day out to the lake. But what I do remember was trying to keep up with Daddy by attempting to walk in his tracks.

The snow was up to my briefs (or thereabouts) which you can't see because they are buried beneath layers of winter clothes, and I wouldn't show you anyway so you'll have to take my word for it.

Dad was wearing his big black boots. We called these clod-hoppers. Sometimes we would put them on for play. Our knees reached up to about two inches of the height of the boots and we could practically take a few steps before the boot, would start moving.

As Dad walked he left huge deep footprints in the snow. I would put one foot in and try to get my other into the next track.

Big Boots to Fill

The problem was that between his prints were the big berms of snow. I would swing my foot up, and over, or as close to over as I could muster, and slide down into the next print. Further problem was, that left one leg in one track and me straddled over into the next track. So instead of walking as the situation demanded, I was left doing a series of straddles. Progress was decidedly slow. In normal conditions it took three of my steps for one of Dad's. Perhaps I was cut down a bit now due to the deep snow but these berms were wide apart.

I wasn't a whole lot taller than those boots and they quickly began to get way ahead of me. So there was that beautiful lake out there with all those geese, Daddy's big black boots churning the snow ahead of me, and me quickly succumbing to a state of exhaustion trying to keep up.

But I suppose I wasn't much different than any other boy. I strewed and strove to follow his tracks no matter how exhausting and impossible it seemed. Fortunately at four you aren't expected to be at full manhood so I eagerly climbed onto Daddy's back as he hefted me up to give me a piggy back ride the rest of the way to the lake. Although we didn't paddle all around it in a big canoe, I did ride around atop Dad and his big clodhopper boots.

The gaggle of giggleless geese had to fly back and forth for quite a few seasons before I could fit Dad's boots well enough to avoid taking a few steps before they started moving. Perhaps it will take the rest of my life to fill his boots. But some day I hope to be man enough to fill big clodhopper boots like he did.

See-Saw

Teeter-totters play into most children's lives at one time or another. They did for us, too, out on the farm. I'm sure you have played on some of them in the city parks or school playgrounds. Usually they are planks securely fastened on a fulcrum so they can't slide around or come off. Usually the plank is smooth and painted or has a metal mount. Some, if not most, have a handle you can hold onto to help keep your balance and prevent sliding or being launched off.

See-Saw

Those weren't available to us on the farm, so we made our own, like many children do. We placed a two by eight by twelve foot rough-cut plank on a fifty-five-gallon steel drum laid on its side.

This created some challenges. Since the board wasn't attached to the drum, the drum would sometimes roll and whoever was on the up side would go racing toward the person on the downside, only without catching him because he was racing backwards clutched to the same board. Hopefully you didn't get your fingers pinched or nearly squashed off as you clutched the plank in front of you with your fingers wrapped around the bottom side as it moved over the barrel with your fingers in between.

Also, a rough-cut plank has not been smoothed up by the sawmill. It has a very rough surface so if you slide along it you are likely to pick up some very nasty slivers.

Still, there was an upside to all this. You see, when you sit on the board and grasp it in front of you, and you are only five or six, when you go up and reach the top of the teeter it seems as if you were looking straight down. And sometimes you start to slide down the board towards the one down on the totter. Or, you do a somersault over your head.

But these big splinters in the wood would stick into the sides of your legs and into your hands, sort of pinning you to the plank so you couldn't fall off. This solution wasn't too popular with us, though, as the pain of the slivers outweighed the advantages.

But teeter-tottering was fun. We spent hours doing it. Eventually our fun would be cut short by some accident. Perhaps when you were coming down you got so brave as to let go and then grab on again on the way up, but behind you this time, and then down you went forgetting your fingers are now where the board meets the ground. Ow-whee! Smashed fingers.

So the tyke is hurt and he jumps off, but this is just when the guy way up just peaked, and suddenly without weight on the other end of the plank, this second tyke plunges to the ground and Wham! His tailbone is hammered to the board, and he now realizes that there is a distinct possibility of growing up two inches shorter than he hoped, so he tries to get up, but a large splinter has him stuck to the board, which elicits some very loud howling and requires an older sibling to come to the rescue.

Other times you don't realize the other guy is a lot heavier than you, and you both jump on and whoo-wee you are catapulted up into the air, almost high enough to see into the future, and for just an instant before you come down…Wait, hang on for a moment, keep holding. Stay there in future, and I will tell you a story of a future event, because the boy never leaves the man when he grows up, and this is about when a teeter about tottered me into the ocean.

When Jeremy, Leo, Jake and I were loggers in southeast Alaska, I caught a hermit crab. I caught him, but if he had caught me, I would be in the sea; as it was, I had him, which almost dunked me in anyhow. It happened like this. We were walking down to the beach from the logging camp on a late Sunday afternoon in a right jolly mood, and perhaps were talking about Teeter and Totter, the see-saw twins, but not likely.

See-Saw

We were just walking along talking about this and that and the other thing. You can listen in if you like, but beware not to get mixed up.

Jeremy: Take a look at this.

Leo: It's nice, but is it as nice as that?

Nathaniel: That's good but I think the other thing has a better chance of really making a difference.

Jeremy: But this seems to be better.

Leo: It is better than that. If you compare this with that, that just seems better than this or the other thing.

Nathaniel: But I don't think you can just leave the other thing out. Upon closer examination this other thing seems more of what one would want even after carefully considering this and that.

Jeremy: No I think I'll stick by this. That just won't cut it, and that other thing doesn't even compare.

Nathaniel: Now hold up just a minute. This other thing can not just be left out. After all, the first shall be last and the last shall be first. So since we are discussing this, that, and the other thing, then I think the other thing is actually the most important, and this we'll just have to put last and even possibly abandon that.

As you can see, our small talk was taking a more serious turn as this, that, and the other started to get a little mixed up, when, having reached the beach, I discovered a little hermit crab getting jostled all around by the waves lapping on the sand. He seemed disconcerted as he tried to keep his borrowed house from leaving him homeless. Perhaps he had just moved into bigger quarters and didn't really fit in yet. Anyway, I picked him up, and he retreated as far as he could into his shell. You see, hermit crabs are a poor sort of lot. They don't have their own shell. They have to make their little sea shanty out of a borrowed shell or some other mollusk or sea shell bearing creature when these have shuffled off their mortal coil and left it abandoned.

We continued our walk as I examined this little creature. We walked out over the bay on a sort of log sidewalk that floated on the water. The loggers had chained two logs together side by side, each about three feet in diameter and sixty feet long. These they chained end to end to make long floating walks ending with a plank dock which could rise up and down with the tides. There, out in the bay, boats could be moored to keep them from being dashed on the beach. Well, we meandered out along one of these until we arrived at a dock. A few big logs made up the raft and then sixteen foot long rough cut planks were nailed fast to the logs to make the sturdy platform.

It just so happened that the planks overhung the last log of the raft by about two feet, unbeknownst to me.

By the time we arrived on the dock, we had abandoned talking about this and that and were simply talking about other things, and even those tailed off as we turned to face the shore of the island to remark on the beauty of the blue sky, against which the sun shone glowingly. It was made even more glorious for us

See-Saw

as it meant a break from the incessant rains in southeast Alaska. The sun is a very welcome guest when he arrives.

As we stood on the dock looking landward, the planks ran straight behind us. I still had the little hermit crab in his shell in my hand and after observing him again, I decided to let him go. But I wanted to see what he looked like without his portable house. So I unceremoniously pulled him out, much to his embarrassment.

There he was stark naked for the entire world to see. Even hermits who abandon the world and give up all worldly possessions have an enveloping garment. But this little hermit crab was forbidden even a modicum of dress in which to hide his nakedness. I couldn't discern the extreme shame of this little crab, as they are by nature red, and so the blushing is not apparent in them. Regardless, either because of his discomfiture in this most awkward moment or because I was afraid to get pinched in his claw, I plopped him shell-less into the bay.

The water was clean but had a hint of blue green in it. Cold, Alaskan salt water. We were about two or three feet up off the water so the crab gave a soft plop as he hit and began to sink. He sank ever deeper. And as he sank, the outgoing tide drifted him towards the dock. The deeper he got the more he drifted under the dock and the closer I edged towards the edge of the plank. Soon my toes, encased in heavy logging boots, hung precipitously on the edge. I leaned even further out so I could keep my eyes on my embarrassed hermit drifting faster under the dock about thirty feet deep or more and almost out of sight. Just when prudence dictated I straighten so as not to fall in, the plank I was standing on shot up in the air behind me.

The nails holding the plank had rusted away in the salt water and left the plank loose. My end went down, and the other went up. I was at the bottom of the teeter and the totter was on the top. And in that wink of an eye my arms flew up and out. As I saw the water rising towards me, my whole mental and physical being switched from a warm fuzzy feeling of contentment to bracing for the frigid, wet, reality of hitting the cold, salty water. There was no going back. A vague salute of a little hermit, exited from the stage, left me alone, suspended between sky and water.

Suddenly, swoosh, I was jerked upward and backwards so fast that I nearly lost my head. The very next second I was standing firmly on the dock as if nothing had happened. The shock of returning to normalcy was almost as hard on my system as when I anticipated hitting the water. I stood stunned. Somehow, as I leaned farther and farther out, Leo and Jeremy had been standing next to me. As the plank I was standing on shot up into the air and I was thrust towards the sea, they both reached out and grabbed me. How they were ever quick or strong enough to jerk me back up and onto the dock I don't know. Their muscles, hardened in the rigors of logging, and their lightning quick response to my peril (don't want to leave out my angel) kept me from meeting the sea. An inch between me and he, that sea, and the next moment, dry as you please.

Well, I assure you I wasn't talking about just this or that or anything else. I was reduced to pretty much jabbering about how

See-Saw

in the world I hadn't just taken a very unpleasant dunk into the frigid, clean, salty bay with all my clothes on.

The plank straddled on the logs had made a perfect teeter totter, and as I went down, it went up. I can't help wondering: As that little hermit was swept out to sea, did he see me and tell his story to his progeny, as I now tell mine to you?

Yep, our teeter-totters roughed us up a bit. You learned not to hold your tongue between your teeth as the other guy got off in case you plummeted to the ground and bit your tongue when your rump hit the ground. You learned not to slide around or you were sure to get a splinter in your hinter end. And you learned that a simple child's toy could pretty near launch you into the future if you got on with someone very much bigger than yourself.

Jumping Jehosaphat and All That

"Jumping Jehoshaphat! What was that?" my electrified brain shouted. How would I know? I don't even know who or what one is. Is it male or female? Fiend or friend? Or is it just a fat Jehosa? You bet I wasn't standing there trying to figure it out, although I lost a second or two in shock before I got started. I jumped, and then I ran. Fast.

I had been walking down the road towards the house in pitch darkness, when all of a sudden a bloodcurdling yell erupted right

Jumping Jehosaphat and All That

behind me and I could hear the gravel crunching as something ran at me. We didn't have a yard light, so the only artificial light was emanating in a soft, yellow, inviting glow from the window of the house.

"Ahhhh!!" I screamed in mortal fear as I sprinted towards the safety of the house. Another screech from behind assailed me. As I ran faster, the fear increased, which goaded me on to an even faster effort. Problem was, my feet couldn't quite keep up with my head. As my eyes locked onto the light in the window and safety, my brain shrieked, "Run! Run!" The window beckoned frantically to my fear besotted mind. My will wanted, but no more power could be cajoled from my legs. It was as if a rubber band had been thrown from the house around the back of my head and propelled me home, but by now I was about to bite the dust. My feet couldn't keep up with my speed, and I was reduced to overextended running while trying not to topple forward. It didn't help that my imagination had now multiplied the yells from behind me by factor ten plus two, and I knew I would get dead real fast if my feet didn't catch up with my head. Just in time, the corner of the house arrived, which I grabbed in desperation as I rounded to home. It caught me and jerked me upright again so I could run the last few steps to the back door.

I nearly ripped the screen door off its hinges as I grasped the handle, jerked it open, and burst into the house. An entry strongly discouraged in normal circumstances, but a necessity in my present state of terror.

My heart had barely made up the beats it had skipped, when Andy and Leo followed me in, laughing to bust a gut at my most ungainly flight.

For yes, it had been Leo and Andy who had conspired to scare the pants off me. And that would have been quite the kafuffle! Just imagine if I had stolen around the house one way, depending entirely on a piece of elastic holding my skivvies up, and crashed into my pants as they came around the other side. As it happened my pants stayed with me and I made it into the house fully breeched.

Leo and Andy had snuck up the road and waited in the dark to scare me. It worked. But perhaps it wouldn't have worked so well if a different exclamation had zinged through my imagination. Instead of "Jumping Jehosaphat! What was that?" what if I had said, "Jumping Jack Sprat! What was that?" A jumping Sprat just doesn't sound very scary even if named Jack, and the chance of him being big and scary when we know he could eat no fat just doesn't figure, though whether his wife could eat no lean seems hardly to bear on our story. Still, I probably would not have been scared if surprised merely with a Sprat instead of getting into a fearsome fright with a fat Jehosa.

Now all of this about jumping Jehosaphats and Sprats like that came about because fourteen siblings, no night lights, forty acres of animal shelters, barbed wire and electric fences made a kid right jumpy. Leo and Andy were always good for a night attack. Ivan would sneak out of the house before I went out with the milk pail at night, and then he'd leap out from the clothesline

Jumping Jehosaphat and All That

pole in near pitch darkness. Cecilia liked to wait in the shadows to boo at my back just as I was turning the handle to enter the house. And now and again I'd walk into an electric fence that seemed to have moved ten feet nearer than it was before, just to give me an electrifying encounter in the dark. All these surprises tended to fray the nerves.

To have your pants depart in the shroud of darkness is a little better than a naked jaybird in the daylight. Still, if when you're running for the safety of the house, your pants streak off in terror in the opposite direction and leave you bursting into the house in all your aboriginal glory well, that's a frightening prospect. A jaybird bursting into the house is quite startling in itself, but a naked one could be catastrophic in a family who even dresses the lettuce.

So it was that our farm created many such fantastical creatures as Jumping Jahosaphats, Jack Sprats and Holy Cows in response to our overstimulated imaginations and the darkness.

Down Under

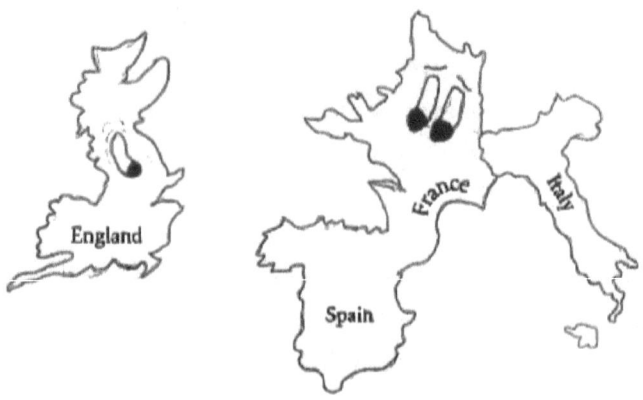

We saw a lot of interesting things when we were "down under." Crawdads, periwinkles, skipping rocks, perhaps a lost coin were there down under. But I never went so deep as to hit Australia.

You have probably heard of down under. I've been told it refers to Australia, located on the map of the globe *under* the equator. But I'm not so sure it's always been there. You see, in seventh grade science class I learned about something called "continental drift." This is the claim that the continents, all seven of them, are still drifting apart, or at least leaving for other seas.

Down Under

This, I am pretty sure, is true. I quite well remember when England sat directly west of France. This is when I was about eleven. You other Elevens's are most likely nodding your heads in hearty agreement. The rock of Gibraltar was between Spain and France, not between Morocco and Spain where it presently resides. And of course the boot of Italy had not kicked Sicily nearly so far into the Mediterranean as it floats now. And Australia, with its kangaroos, was quite pleased with itself sitting between Africa and South America. That is what drove Madagascar mad. It wanted South America all to itself, not pushed up against Africa.

My grade school teachers tried to keep up as well as they could with all these continents drifting around. This made geography class very interesting.

Sister Mary would pull the large rollup map of the world down from its roll up over the chalkboard and display the world and all its wonderful lands. There would be England sitting squarely above France. And lo! By the time I took my geography test, England had drifted down to live nearly beside France to the west, and there I would place it on my test map paper. But would it stay? No. When my test paper would be plunked down on my desk there would be a big red X through England with an arrow pointed to the North. And even Scotland and Ireland would have switched places by the time I took my test.

And the hapless Christopher Columbus would have most assuredly made it to spicy India and avoided that unceremonious crash into North America if that huge continent had stayed put and not drifted into his charted path.

How to Skin a Skunk

How many other school children lost their way around the world like I did in Geography class?

Take Hawaii for example. Well you have to take it; they're not going to just give it to you. When you looked at a map of the United States there was Hawaii floating just off the coast of California, with a big black square scribed around it so you couldn't miss it. And Alaska, what was it doing in that big black square sitting in the Gulf of Mexico? Come test time when I placed those states where they were sitting when I memorized the map, I got the test back with a big arrow pointed way up above Seattle. There Sister placed Alaska hooked on to the far northwest corner of Canada.

As for Hawaii, it was not even within sight of California. It had drifted thousands of miles out to sea. And she had the globe to prove it. Oh, I know they aren't continents, but they were just as drifty. Ask any eleven year old how many geography tests were failed because the states had moved around from where they were before the test was taken.

Thankfully, all this continental drift seemingly has slowed down a bit. The older I get, the more the continents seem to pretty much stay put. Although come to think of it, is Australia still down under? It's a long time since I looked.

Lookout Hike

There was to the southwest of us a Forest Service lookout station. We could only see it if we were way up in the field far away from the house. The lookout stood upon a hilltop about four miles the way the crow flies. The mountain of the whole range of hills, on which the lookout was, was the tallest that ran alongside the Big Spokane River. The Forest Service had located the lookout post on the mountain top so that forest fires could be spotted, reported and hopefully contained. The lookout itself was a wooden structure with virtually all glass walls. It was perched atop wooden stilts sixty feet in the air or so. It was accoutered such that a Ranger could live there for the fire season with food supplies and water brought up by others at intervals.

We hiked from our house to the station a number of times just for the fun of it.

One fine, sunny summer day, Jake, Jeremy, and I and a neighbor boy John started out for the lookout. After crossing a few fields and traversing a woodlot, we came across a dirt road that we could walk on for awhile. Just before leaving the woods for the road we had refreshed ourselves by swimming in a small pond. It was most magical. A small pool was formed by a rock formation as a small creek burbled through field and wood.

We were in high spirits as we followed the dirt road through the trees, when Jake spotted a huge wasp nest hanging from a fir branch that reached out over the road. It was about twenty feet up off the ground, and looked like a great big grape bunch hanging invitingly from the branch.

One would think that having reached the age of reason a few years before, we would have had some common sense stored up or at least a few pints of it if gathered from all four of us. But somehow a beautiful picture had formed in our imaginations of a most interesting adventure.

A huge wasp nest hung over a country road, and a beautiful sunny morning was in the making. Wonderful throwing rocks lying in lazy slumber, awakened by the chatter of boys, looked forward with eager anticipation to being thrown. A road to run on without obstacles stretched before us.

Lookout Hike

Wasps that were no longer than our thumbknuckle to thumbnail lived there. Their eyes just specks within their heads meant their tiny eyes would never know what direction a hail of rocks came from. Right? And perhaps the fact that there wasn't a thimbleful of commonsense near made a perfect setup.

So we started looking for throwing rocks. Some rocks were disappointed as we tossed them away, rejected. We wanted just the right size, weight and grip surface. About three apiece would do. The lucky stones we kept were held, two in the left and one in the right hand. We then assayed the nest. The huge bulb had a hole in the bottom where the worker wasps were busy egressing and ingressing. Guard bees hung around on the cone.

Next we planned our assault. We figured that with four of us firing, we could get off a very quick volley of rocks from about twenty feet away. We figured they would not see us throwing. We decided that on the count of one, two, three, we would all wind up and let loose. We eagerly anticipated the smacking of at least three or four rocks into the nest, exploding it into pieces while we watched a swarm of angry wasps erupt into the air. A perfect bee blast. No, I hadn't learned a thing from the experience of being chased by angry honeybees into Mrs. Hickelgruber's brambles.

So we all lined up and yelled in unison, "One, two, three!" and heaved ho. An array of projectiles winged towards the nest, some smashed into the nest and ripped it wide open, and a large piece plunged to the ground. A colossal cloud of wasps erupted into the air.

How to Skin a Skunk

I don't know if the queen left her throne or not, but I know it took less than a second for the nurse bees to arrest the spoons of food that were advancing towards the hungry mouths of her pupas or pappooses (I did not have time to determine which) and chuck the chuck. The nurses were commandeered to join the guards in their yellow jackets as they were all well equipped with stingers to wreak vengeance on whomever had assaulted their fortress.

But what we found out in a real hurry was that hornets have a tiny eye that must see with mega-vision. We hardly had time to snap up our dropped jaws, unhinged at our shock at seeing such a huge swarm of hornets explode about, when before we could turn and run, the hornets were upon us.

We ran for our very lives. They were coming after us with very bad thoughts. Very bad thoughts indeed. Vengeful thoughts. A deadly sin that ought to have caused them to pause. But did it? No immortal souls had they, so the threat of Death, Judgment, Heaven and Hell had no stopping power for them. Fortunately there were so many of them cursing us all at the same time that distinctive words could not be heard. What we did hear was a hum of a gazillion angry wasps. This saved the damage to our souls if we had heard the actual words flung at us, but did not spare us the very real danger of the harm our bodies were going to suffer if they caught us.

None of us were ignorant of the pain of a wasp sting, and the thought of having thousands of these little poisoned darts poke into our anatomy spurred us on to warp-like speeds. I made up

Lookout Hike

for a speed deficit, being the skinniest, by being the scaredest, and kept up with the faster bigger boys as we swept down that country lane in a blur of wind and dust.

We ran up the hills and streaked down the vales, we flew by the fences as we swatted our tails. Our vamoosing left the bovines, the houses and the gooses standing gaping in perplexion. Flapping and flailing we fled dead ahead until we were winded and the wasps had chased us from their territory. Our lungs were plumb played out and our legs weakened so that we flopped down on the side of the road to take a breather and take account of damage done.

What we were shocked to find out was that only our pride had been stung. Any dignity that we might have started out with was left littered over a country mile of graveled road in a most sissified flight. Since you can't get a good look at yourself even in the best of circumstances, being a blurred dynamo of speed made it completely impossible, so we spent our time laughing at each other as we poked fun at whomever seemed to look the most ridiculous in that mad run. We marveled at how many wasps had burst from the nest and how instantaneously they had attacked.

We were a bit of a disheveled bunch as we continued on our way to the lookout and beyond.

The beyond entailed descending a two hundred foot, very steep sand bank that dropped down to the Big Spokane River, on the backside of the hills of the mountain where the lookout stood. We wanted to swim in the river before we started on our way home. The sandbank was so steep that it afforded us a thrilling opportunity to do some serious sand sliding. By jumping up and forward, we could fly a good ten feet or more before we hit the bank much further down, and since it was so slanted, when we hit the dirt it gave way in a big avalanche beneath us as we slid further. Then up for another jump and sail and slide until hot, sweaty and very dusty, we reached the bottom of the hillside and ran to the river. We raised a raucous ruckus in the river water that would have made a dancing pod of killer whales proud. Unfortunately that river water also filled up the thimble that held our common sense, thereby diluting it even more.

It was all fun soaking wet in the river but it started to sink into our minds that we would have to scale back up that two hundred foot sand bank and hike that forest and field all the way back home.

And the sandbank did give us a struggle. Having beaten the sand out of our shoes when we got to the bottom before our swim, we tied the shoe-laces together and slung them over our shoulders on the way up to avoid refilling them with sand and having to lift twenty pounds as we picked up our feet for each step.

So up we started to scale. Problem was, every time you lifted your foot up, you slid back down in the loose sand half a foot. It made for exhaustingly slow upward progress.

We used branches from bushes we could at times grab to help pull up on. This would hold us and stop us from sliding. Trouble was if we broke one or lost our grip we ended up upsetting the sand even more and then we'd slide way back down.

Lookout Hike

As now, when I slipped backwards and my hand began to lose its grip, so I swung widely and grabbed the bank with my other hand. Having saved my fall with my hand fully grupped there, in desperation I formed my loose hand to get another grip, but just then Noah Webster objected that grupped is not a word. I wasn't about to let go just to get my grammar right. Sometimes grupping, although having an unpleasant sound, has to be used. A griping Webster is not enough persuasion to give up your grip. You just have to hang on as best you can.

If you gotta grupp, even if Webster gripes, he has to, at the least, leave you long enough there, so you can get a better grip.

We finally made it to the top, but by now we were so hot that looking back at the river was a lot more inviting than our three mile hike home. Yet hike we must. We were not up to another hiker versus hornets race, so we went through an extra field to avoid the area of the angry wasps. Perhaps it prepared us to pack a little more common sense in our pockets the next time.

Drowning Worms

There is an industry devoted to supplying a multitude of youngsters and grownups alike with all they need to practice their avocation, drowning worms. Primitive records show this activity as having very petrified roots. A stick, horsehair, a chip of sharp broken bone and a worm, all attached to each other, have been identified.

Like with most outdoor activities, Leo introduced us littler fellows.

The unfortunate souls who have never had the pleasure of drowning worms, or who have only listened to advertisements

Drowning Worms

of the aforesaid, have called this activity fishing. Now it is true that a worm drowner will at times, in fits of sarcasm, call his avocation fishing, and the uninitiated will then call the activity by that name.

How the name fishing came to be attached to the noble enterprise came about as follows.

A worm drowner, a look of quiet satisfaction overcoming his countenance in anticipation of a thoroughly drowned worm, is jolted from his gentle reverie into a frantic grab at his drowner pole as its tip plunges towards the water and his pole is nearly jerked from his hands. He yells, "A fish!" in obvious overexcitement.

Imagine, if you will, yourself in this predicament. You have just spent two hours getting a worm thoroughly soaked. You have even retrieved him from the watery depths a few times to be sure he hasn't escaped. And when on close inspection you have detected movement, you have carefully lowered him back into the deep, when suddenly a fish shatters the tranquility that your satisfied soul has achieved.

You are thrust into a fight with a fish. With extreme emotion you scream to your partners, "Get the net! Get the net!" There's no way you're going to let this fish get away. You're bound and determined he'll land in your freezer. You'll take no chance that he'll live again to challenge your worm drowning dreams. The bigger the fish, the bigger your enthusiasm as you anticipate hanging that fish on the wall to show every other drowner that you've just cleared the lake of a monstrous fish daring to disturb the peace. In charity, you must keep the fish from foiling other worm drowner dreams.

Since worm drowning is such a sacred rite, it is done for hours at a time with great solemnity. So, when the somewhat rare appearance of a fish enters the picture, the scene is fraught with great emotion. "Wow, a fish!" one exclaims. The bigger the fish, the more emotable the drowner. "Wow, look at that humongous monster!" he shouts.

Because of these experiences, worm drowners have come up with a word to describe this incredible interruption.

Here's how it works: "What are you doing? Drowning worms?" asks one drowner as he passes another, in seeming nonchalance.

"Naw, just fishing," the other replies laconically. "Haven't gotten but a few of these worms drowned. Keep catching these here little fish," as he pats a huge Largemouth Bass, keeping company with other large fish. "Probably caught them all out of this here part of the lake, so I'll just keep drowning worms here."

Since catching fish while drowning worms is somewhat rare, when it does happen, it is derisively called "fishing".

Consequently, when a man leaves his wife to cleave to his fishing tackle, and the wife ask in her ignorance, "Where are you going?" and he says, "Fishing," she knows to put on a steak for dinner. He'll be late drowning worms. So, sarcasm, by usage, has just become a common name now. Fishing.

This principle can be applied equally well to other aspects of the more general art of angling. Worms can be very effective at

Drowning Worms

cleaning lakes of seaweed, even hatching salmon eggs. Webster went fishing once and he found that the tackle used in drowning worms (reels, rods, lines, sinkers,) worked for these other activities also, so he made up the word angling to encompass them all. And so angling got put into his dictionary.

The art of angling spawned a whole business of those who supply hooks, plugs, lines, flask, even ... flies.

They have huge plugs shaped like fish, frogs, newts, and, yes, worms to help dredge seaweed from lake bottoms. Can't escape fishing altogether even here though. Sometimes a seaweed dredge will have dredged in quite a respectable boatload of seaweed over the length of the day, almost making the thousands of dollars worth of fancy equipment worth it when, without warning, a massive hunk of fish flesh like a bass or pike will get hooked, and the angler with extreme agitation will pull the pike or bass into the boat, with great huffing and puffing. You bet he'll put it away in the freezer or hang it on the wall as a trophy. A lesson to fish everywhere not to do that again! Do not disturb the dredge!

Jeremy was one such unfortunate fellow. It's painful to me now, many years later, to tell you how bad I felt for him, he catching all those fish. I didn't suffer so. Fish seldom interrupted my worm drowning and seaweed clearing. Jeremy, on the other hand, could scarcely drown any worms before a fish would get hooked and we all had to reel in our lines so he could play the fish and get it into the boat where it couldn't do any more harm.

How to Skin a Skunk

One day, Jeremy, myself, Andy, and Leo went fishing on a perfect day for drowning worms. We got up very early. It was late April, and a cold dreary rain greeted us as we latched to the top of the car the 16 foot flat bottom canoe that Leo and Andy had built in the living room. The worms would be nearly drowned before they were even plunked into the lake.

We thought a day out on a gray lake with gray skies pouring buckets of gray rain into a blue boat with four soggy fishermen would be great fun. Not to be. Our fun was cut short all on account of Jeremy.

As we settled into a nice rhythm, I got four if not five very nice worms drowned and no fish even dared bite. Andy and Leo serenely cast and re-cast their lines in a beautiful cadence as fat, skinny, long and squirmy worms flew overhead to be plonked into the lake without even a curious look by the fish.

But when Jeremy cast his line we would repeatedly hear "I got a bite!" And we would glance at each other with disgusted looks, which meant "He *would* ruin our fun." And then "I got one!" would ring out.

"You mean you finally got one drowned?" we would ask hopefully.

"No, I got another fish." And sure enough another beautiful trout would come flashing into the boat.

This got very tiresome for us three as we had to keep pulling in our fishing lines. How can you drown a worm well if he spends more time in the boat than in the water?

Drowning Worms

Even the State has put a limit on this discourteous behavior. You can only catch six fish for the day. Therefore, if one fisherman like Jeremy dominates the activity, the State feels that there is compelling interest to stop this for the sake of the comity of the worm drowners.

Well, as we sat soaking up the liquid sunshine this fine day, Jeremy rudely interrupted us four times and beached four lusty trout into the bottom of the boat. I was on my way to drowning a tolerable number of worms as we approached lunch, when Andy's reveries were cut short twice by two fish who insisted in joining their fellows in the boat. Leo had less time to drown his as he paddled around in the canoe with the vain hope that different parts of the lake drowned worms better than others. He hoped to avoid the nuisance of pesky fish. Besides Jeremy intermittingly interrupting this endeavor, he was quite successful. The rest of us were very avoided by any fish.

Hatching salmon eggs by dangling them in the water on a hook is not all that unreasonable I suppose, but I never was good at it, never got it to happen. Still I tried often enough. The idea is to bypass the whole business of a salmon having to emerge from some egg lodged in a stream bed in faraway Alaska or a Columbian tributary, then having to trek down turbulent waters to the ocean, with a little sightseeing with the whales and back up the same river past the grasping jaws and claws of grizzly bears where it might find a drowning worm. All this could be bypassed by simply putting the salmon egg on a hook and waiting for it to hatch there. I have seen anglers sit for hours, even days, waiting for fish to appear on their lines. Some have sitten so long that the lake freezes over. Some even build little huts on the ice where they sit for months trying to hatch that egg. They call these ice fishermen.

Does it work? Sort of. The eggs do hatch. Trout, cutthroats, perch and pike will burst into life on the end of the line. But I have never seen a salmon emerge.

Back the boat up for a moment. Why did Webster call all this activity angling?

Anglers are so called because of the peculiar slouch that a fisherman has, when he mopes about the house trying to do all the honey-dos before he is let out of the house. When his knuckles are pretty near dragging on the ground in dejection and there is hardly enough life in him to slouch to the couch, his wife ejects him from the home with the most beautiful words he could hear. "The bloodhound's face looks downright cheerful next to yours. What's the matter with you?" and he, barely able to scrape his eyelids off the floor, replies "I need to drown worms."

"How can that be?" she says. "The last time you tried it you ended up with a bunch of slimy fish in my bathtub. Now you can go, but no more fishing."

You have probably gathered how serious a business this is: this drowning of worms and cleaning the lake with fishhooks.

One particularly good day for drowning worms (yes, it was raining hard), we came back to the boat launch in the canoe

Drowning Worms

and there were the most serious and downcast bunch of worm-drowners you ever saw lolligating about.

Says one to another with a downright hang-dog look, "How many did you get drowned?"

Says him back with a little shrug of disgust and disinterest, "Couldn't get but a few drowned. Before I could even get one respectably waterlogged, this here two foot, twelve-pound rainbow trout grabbed on and wouldn't let go. Had to fight him over forty minutes." He has to shift his weight a little as he hoists up a stringer of four huge trout, dipping his head in shame. "After all that fighting I lost a good worm. Then this here ten-pounder latched on and burnt up another fifteen minutes and darned if what with the others that kept getting hooked, I lost pert near the whole day just getting these fish off my line."

Even at my young age I could feel his pain, all that effort in catching worms and only getting a few drowned.

The first says back, as he tries to hide his four-pounder, six-pounder, and yes, eight-pounder, behind his back, "I know, I got a few drowned more than you but these pesky trout just wouldn't let me alone."

What brightened them both up, and their delight spread quickly through the rest of us standing at the boat-launch, was coming towards us.

"See that feller over there, now he's done real well."

And we did look, and there was a sight to behold, a worm-drowner who had dedicated himself to cleaning up the lake. He had a pile of seaweed stacked in the back of his boat; it hung over the side, and the real joy was that his engine was thoroughly wrapped in old fishing line, seaweed strings, an ancient anchor rope, and a styrofoam lid from a discarded cooler. Now that was success. Not a fish in sight.

That really seemed to deflate the fourth guy there. He shrugged and hitched his string of huge trout into his truck.

"I'll be seeing you guys, got to get these home and cleaned out and into the freezer before my wife sees them. She's warned me that if I don't get more worms drowned and if I keep filling her freezer with fish, she's not going to let me go anymore. So long, fellers, better luck next time."

Well we felt pretty bad for those so-called fishermen. They sure couldn't drown worms if they tried. We felt good, though, as not many more than a few whole and a few half worms remained in our can. We drowned nearly every one of them. And there were plenty more left on the farm for our next worm drowning adventure.

Skunk Story

A crowd of youngsters swirled around Leo's Dodge Dart as it rolled into the yard. Jeremy was driving. I was riding shotgun (a glorified title for the person who has to get out and get the gate). As we climbed out it became obvious that another smell intermingled with the swirling. It was distinct, it certainly stank, and what stank was soon discovered to be skunk, undeniably. What stinked, stank, and stunk was a dead skunk that I had surreptitiously picked up on the highway. I had shoved it into a garbage bag and flung it into the trunk of the car before any

How to Skin a Skunk

cars came by to see us, or my stomach had a chance to jump out and run for the woods. I was certain the skunk smell would empty that delicious ham sandwich, so nicely packed by Rose and eaten with relish, just an hour before.

I had been practicing my hand at taxidermy; so far I had stuffed a chipmunk and a chickadee. A moose I thought should be my next attempt. No moose had offered its services and lo! There in the middle of the road a skunk had left its mortal remains.

The sulfurous smell seemed to belie the argument that animals don't have an immortal soul, for where did that hellish smell come from if he didn't have one? As it was, I just snatched his earthly carcass so I could have his hide.

"Did you guys hit a skunk?" asked Peter with his nose pinched shut.

"Jeremy took his shoes off," Ivan suggested with a smirk. It was pretty embarrassing. Usually the interesting thing about bringing home game was the story that surrounded it. Heroic and bold actions were related with great aplomb and the admiring sighs were drunk in with swelling pride and delight.

But how to tell a tale of the taking of a dead skunk? Scooping of dead skunks would surely be met with laughter, hooting and derisive humor. Who would ever be stupid enough to pick up a dead skunk?

Well, there was no use embellishing the facts. So to put an end quickly to the mounting excitement and as Dad rounded the house with the ever increasing aroma thickening around us, I quickly said to all interested parties with pinched noses that

Skunk Story

I had scooped a dead skunk off the highway so I could skin it and keep the hide. This was met with great skepticism, and the crowd quickly dispersed to remote destinations around the farm. I was left alone.

To effect my design, I chose a spot northwest of the house to do the skinning. I hooked a little cross stick up on the power pole for a skinning rack. Even I was amazed at just how badly the skunk scent got out of the black plastic garbage bag. I didn't have any respirators or gas masks, so I just took my handkerchief and tied it around my nose like a common bandit.

I then opened the trunk and got my bag of skunk and ran over to the pole. I dumped him unceremoniously out of the bag and tied two old shoestrings onto his bare feet to hang him on the cross stick.

I got him hung up alright and got out my pocket knife and commenced skinning. I quickly learned that there was a lot of difference between smelling a skunk from the inside of a car doing fifty-five miles an hour down the highway and having your nose just eighteen inches away from a smell that can repel bears, cougars, and wolves that have approached with little good intent.

As my skinning progressed, my eyes began to sting a little, my throat began to tighten and mutiny was brewing in the recesses of my innards. By the time I got to his head I was sick. Problem was that this is the hardest and most detailed part to skin. I had to get my own head in real close to see, I had to go very slowly and make very little and delicate cuts.

How to Skin a Skunk

A few times I had to quit and run away where there was a breeze to get some unpolluted air sucked into my lungs. Wasn't easy though. When you're that close to your odiferous friend, his perfume hangs onto you and follows you all about. I would run out and gasp for some fresh air, get a huge lungful and hold my breath, run back to the skunk, do some skinning, and then burst out the used air and run for some more.

Problem was, this started making me lightheaded, so I had to be quick, not get sick. The handkerchief did virtually nothing. The offending odor seemed to come under, go over and just waft right through it. I suppose it did disguise from outsiders who the idiot was skinning the skunk.

Need I say there were no volunteers around to help relieve me from my distress? Chores that had seemed irksome at other times seemed downright pleasant to them now. Even the pigpen seemed like a field of clover to play in.

I was nearly at the end of my task and determined to finish what I had begun. But I was in a race with the rising nausea about to overwhelm me. I had gotten the front feet skinned out, had maneuvered around the ears and eyes some, and I'd even done the lips. But now what was in me wanted out of me, and I was feeling so sick through my whole being I just had to quit. I had intended to change my strings around so I could skin out the hind feet, having then the hide in its entirety. But now, nearly fainting, I just cut the skin off at the feet and flung it into a bucket.

With that I set out for a long walk to get some fresh air. I walked nearly up to the mailbox and back and got some of the

Skunk Story

wobbliness out of my legs. I had read in one of my adventure books that tomato juice would take skunk smell out of clothes or off dogs or June bugs, but I didn't know for sure. First I went and got a shovel and dug a deep hole in the woods and buried the skinned out carcass. What the worms did with it I don't know, you'll have to read all about it in the *Worm Gazette* article: Willie Worm Meets Skinned Skunk.

After this I had Ivan get me a quart sized can of tomato sauce from Mom and after having cut off the top with the can opener he so kindly remembered, I had Ivan pour some over my hands and pocket knife, while letting it drain into the bucket with the skin in it. After washing my hands and knife in it he dumped the rest into the bucket on top of the skunk hide. With a stick I stirred it around, thoroughly. I saturated that hide with tomato sauce. Then I got Ivan to get me some clean clothes and I hightailed it into the woods, where I changed. I left the foul clothes hanging in a tree until they lost their offending odor. The skunk smell was slowly dissipating from the farm. By the time I got the clothes hung in the woods, the carcass buried, my hands washed and the hide drenched in tomato juice, nary a whiff remained. Kids started returning, minus pinched noses, and the whole farm resumed some normality. It was a week or so before Leo's car lost all of its tell-tale smell though.

It was astonishing to us that the tomato juice had eliminated all the smell from my hands and knife. So it was with great expectations that I lifted the lid on the bucket with the hide in it

How to Skin a Skunk

in the morning. Again, to my amazement there was virtually no smell in the bucket.

I gave the hide a thorough wash under the outside faucet. I stretched it out and held it up to behold the beautiful black skunk skin with the broad white stripe. My smelly adventure had yelt a wonderful pelt.

I tanned it with a mixture of alum and salt. When it was nearly dry I assiduously worked Neat's foot oil into the hairless side of it. It turned out to be a beautifully tanned hide. It has hung on my walls throughout these many years and has elicited many very quizzardly questions, even some as odd as: What does quizzardly mean? Well, you'll know when you skin a skunk. But you skin the skunk. I, a Skink, I think. They don't stink.

He Swallowed the Whole Thing!

I might have mentioned it before. If I have, I won't mention it. But if I haven't, I'll tell you now.

Dad had gotten thirty or so concrete pipe sections about three feet long and three feet in diameter. He eventually used some to line the thirty foot deep hand dug well when the wooden shoring had deteriorated. The rest he stood on end next to each other to make pens. For many years the boar was kept in one, and years later Dad moved them to make a cattle corral.

At the time of this tale they were the boar's pen. The upturned pipes made great forts that we could pop down into to play. This time Jeremy and I decided to commandeer one pipe for a snake and frog pen. The pipes were ideal for this, so heavy they sunk a little into the ground. And nothing could push under them and most critters couldn't jump their three-foot height. We carefully arranged a layout for our repti-amphib friends and now had to acquire the occupants.

This time we headed to the Big Stream, two miles the way the crow flies across forest and vale. We took along some used bread sacks to carry our captives back.

It was a lovely day for hunting these critters. Even so, snakes are a little shy about boys with bread sacks. This snake shyness kept us from having the delight of one coming out of the bushes and jumping in when we strolled by.

So after hours of searching through the tall grasses along the stream, we were able to scare out only a nice two foot water snake, a beautiful black with the fine yellow stripe down his back. Now we had lunged and grabbed and missed and jumped and twisted trying to grasp that fleeing snake. Looked a little silly: like barefoot fleas on a hot skillet. But one couldn't argue with the results. It was a nice snake. Don't remember how we caught the frog; he doesn't either, as you will see.

We weren't going to keep our small bullfrog in with the snake when we put them into their pens, but we saw no harm in tossing the frog into the sack with the snake to get it home. We had put a little water into the sack to keep these little critters from drying out. The bread sack was mostly clear plastic with some painted on labeling, so we could see them in there a little.

He Swallowed the Whole Thing!

After we had rounded up our catch we started for home.

A bit later we were crossing a meadow on the backside of the Big Hill when Jeremy stopped and opened the bag to take a peek in and see how our critters were faring.

"What?!" he gasped.

Startled, I grabbed the edge of the bag and pulled it towards me so I could see what was so startling.

The snake had swallowed the frog's left hand. At first I just thought it was a friendly handshake. A reptile to amphib intro. A left-handed handshake?

I couldn't believe it either. With all our frog and snake experiences we had never seen a snake swallow anything. Mostly, I suppose because our snakes escaped wherever we tried to pen them in before they needed to eat. Thus, we always thought snake dining took place in some quiet, dark place where they wouldn't be disturbed or frightened.

"You think it's trying to eat it?" I asked Jeremy incredulously.

He looked again, doubtfully.

"Probably just bit it in fright, being jolted and squished up with the frog." We closed it up and continued walking; we just couldn't believe we might witness a snake swallowing something. After a couple hundred more yards we peeked in again. Sure enough, the snake was swallowing it. Even in that very chaotic environment. The snake had now swallowed the frog's whole arm.

"Wow!" we both exclaimed. "It *is* eating it!" We hurried towards home faster. Now how, we thought, could the snake continue swallowing the frog? Headfirst is the only sensible way we supposed but how to effect that? Well, we took a peek again about a mile farther on. We were really hurrying so we could dump it into the pen and watch the whole nature thing in fullness. But to our dismay the snake had unhooked its jaw joint and had worked the frog's head by a movement of the left cheek. It was getting the frog more in. This was almost too much excitement to contain. By now we were practically running, on our own road half way down to the house. At the mine's pump house we stopped and looked in again, and lo and behold the snake had turned that frog and had already swallowed its left arm and head. By the time we got all the way home and looked in, there were only the hind legs sticking out of that now very bigheaded snake.

One, we never knew snakes would eat in public --especially in such a violent atmosphere. And two, we didn't know they could unhinge the jaw to swallow something two or three times their natural mouth and throat size. We watched in awe, gazing into that old bread sack, as the snake finished swallowing the whole frog and its legs disappeared into the snake's mouth.

Perhaps you are thinking "Poor frog." But we don't know that. It wasn't carrying any financial statements or papers or such like when we caught it, and anyway even if it were living below the poverty line, I doubt that would have bothered the conscience of the snake.

Goodness, we know of some very ancient ancestors who didn't have a stitch of clothes and a snake beguiled them, perhaps with a little more guile than a handshake, but it didn't stop that snake.

He Swallowed the Whole Thing!

I think that what really happened with our snake was that, as in the case of so many children, the snake just couldn't stop sticking its tongue out at the frog, the frog got tired of it and tried to stuff the tongue back down his throat to stop his impertinence, and his hand got stuck. Then what was the snake to do?

Maybe your experience is like mine. I have never gotten a snake to talk, his hand signs are out of the question, and there are no shoulders on him to shrug as if to say, "Well, what else was I supposed to do?" But Jeremy and I were thrilled that day to see nature in action and we were left with the impression that the snake had a quiet satisfied look on his face which seemed to say, "I can't believe I swallowed the whole thing!"

Chickenpox

One day we were all out sledding in the old mine. I began to feel a little sickish; just extra energerish and other-ishes. Following a good afternoon of this sledding, we started for the house and I felt extra hot.

When we got home, we pulled off our layers of cold weather wrappings and hung them all around the wood stove to dry them out. As I was saying, I was feeling kind of ishish so I went back by the beds and pulled my shirt up to see why I was a little itchy on my stomach. To my chagrin there were a few tiny bubbles under the skin, like little blisters. Well, chickenpox must have

Chickenpox

been going around because I had heard of the little blisters. But here is the part I got mixed up in my young mind. I thought that if I could just get rid of the blisters I could stop from getting chickenpox worse.

So then and there I decided to get rid of them. I plucked them off. This is not the itchy scabs you get after the pox. I was going to nip them in the bud, so to speak. So I pulled off all these little bubbles, only five to ten were there. That seemed to take care of it. This was late afternoon. I eagerly looked again right before bed, and crickets! If there weren't twenty more or so! This was not good, and I set about remedying the situation. Off came these little buggers, just like those I'd plucked off before. Now surely I had this pesky disease confounded. No more pox.

Land sakes alive! I woke up the next morning feeling quite peevish and behold, I was covered with the pox all over, and so was Cecilia. To get rid of this, I would have to be skinned alive. I could see no good in that. My skin had served me quite well up to this point, although it was in revolt now. Besides there wasn't much market for tanned tykes' hides that I knew of, even if some fathers still did the tanning.

Well, as I said, Cecilia commiserated with me in my distress by coming down with chickenpox also, and she was covered all over too. It's possible all the other little ones got it at the same time. I just don't remember.

Oh, but why call them chickenpox? There are chicken pies, chicken stews, broths, boiled, basted, boxed and fried chicken. Cowards are chickens, girls are chicks, and rubber chickens are used in magic shows. And it's still true you can't get full on a plate of chicken lips.

And consider this. For decades chickens quailed under the withering eye of the inquisitor. "Just *why did you* cross the road?"

So there's been a lot of chickenness going around for a long time but I still don't know about the pox part.

We asked Mom. She seemed to know pretty near everything, but even she could not answer this one.

So there we would sit, languishing and moping about when we weren't too feverish, Cecilia and I. And we had to endure not only the progression of the blisters into ever hardening scabs, but the barrage of clucking and squawking noises of teasing siblings reminding us of our plight tied to chickens. We did look rather pathetic. Poxxed and dotted all over. Certainly not a time to go knitting with the knickerbockers gnats. Well that's what fever does to you; you think the craziest thoughts.

There were a few consolations though. Daddy made his homemade eggnog. You know, milk, raw eggs, cinnamon, and nutmeg. It was so good.

Couldn't go to school for a whole week or more too. That was almost worth it in itself. I said almost. Strange thing about getting to stay home when you're sick. Sure, when you dream at school how nice it would be not to be there and maybe you'll get sick and sent home, it all sounds so good. But you forget, when you're sick and get to stay home, you *are* sick. And that's no fun.

Now some might say, yeah, but how about when you are not really so sick? Well, we didn't try to pull that one with Daddy

Chickenpox

and Mom. Good conscience, perhaps, or good parents, (sort of the same thing I guess) kept us from that.

When the itch came, though, oh that was awful. We were told forty-eleven times not to pick the scabs. They'll leave holes that will not go away the rest of your life.

Wow, but how could you keep from doing it? Because all at the same time there would be an itch on your toes and the end of your nose, a tickle on the tummy, and a tease on your knees, a peck on the neck, and a pox in your socks all stretching from morn to nox.

One solution to keep us from scratching these little rascals was that Mom made us wear socks on our hands; what a wonderful thought: chickenpox socks! And that wasn't all. Squirming around as we tried to get away from all this itching earned us the name "spastics," courtesy of Andy.

One of the many advantages of growing up surrounded by a lot of brothers and sisters is that when a disease hits, there are bound to be others who wallow with you in the same misery, thus demonstrating the maxim: a sorrow shared is a sorrow lessened. And then, too, the healthy ones could provide a never-ending stream of humorous disparagement designed to distract the patient from his misery.

Skyhooks

Do you know what a skyhook is?

"If you slip and start to slide down, just grab a skyhook," Leo said with authority in his voice in order to steady our nerves. We were inching our way along a barely discernable trail that led across a sandy sided steep hillside. It was nearly a cliff face. If we did start to slide off this steep trail we would accelerate rapidly down the sand slide and perhaps even tumble to our deaths on the jumble of rocks below.

Skyhooks

Or again, I started across the top of the A frame swing set in imitation of a tightrope walker. Leo had just done it, and was encouraging me to get across. "If you start to fall, just grab a skyhook," he said assuredly.

Another: We were the line of boys who waded across Dragoon Creek, our hands held high over our heads, in which were grasped our shoes and socks and fishing rods. The worms that rode in the tomato cans tied to our waist were in imminent danger of drowning en masse if we slipped into the creek.

It wasn't that the water was so high it was treacherous, it's just that when you wanted to cross and not swim, you had to cross in water no higher than your knees. But the shallower the water was, the swifter it flowed. What with tender feet and hard, somewhat jagged and slippery rocks and rushing current, it was a challenge to stay upright. There was also the threat of stepping into a deep hole that the water had washed out in the bottom of the creek. This could send you down under. "If you lose your balance and start to go under the water, just grab a skyhook!" Leo yelled to project his voice over the rushing current and reach us boys who strung out in the line behind. Can you see a line of skyhooks hanging down over our heads for us to grab? Well we couldn't either, so fortunately we all crossed without incident.

"Grab a skyhook, grab a skyhook!" Leo yelled at Andy, as he pitched over the side of the haystack. There it was again: that assuring, sometimes matter of fact statement, sometimes sudden exhortation when a fall was afoot.

How to Skin a Skunk

Now, the number of times I fell down, multiplied by the number of times Leo, Andy, Jake, Jeremy, Ivan, Peter, Tristan, and Damien fell down (and that's only counting the boys), yet not one of us managed to catch a skyhook, should make you wonder if they really did exist.

Reasonable for sure. But you must consider the evidence for them. Big brothers are older, wiser, and more experienced, and know everything about anything, as we remarked before, notwithstanding the objections of older sisters. Perhaps as little brothers we should have been more circumspect. Just why did Leo himself fall down on occasion if skyhooks were so dependable? Course he never admitted he fell down. Said he was just testing to see if the ground would catch him if he did fall. Now that may be an answer a big sister might be skeptical about, but who had time for objections when you were so busy little brothering?

So first, we have it on the older brother's authority that skyhooks do exist. Second, in almost all falls, we see a very distinct reaching. A few exceptions perhaps, like the genteel or ladylike falls of women who clutch Christmas packages in a tight embrace as they gently fall over into a snowdrift. Or a lady as she slides gently down the side of a husband when he flails around trying to stay upright on a slippery piece of ice. But, most falls entail a very distinct reaching.

The reaching can be an almost instantaneous stiff arm to the sky or an opened hand upward push and a closed fist shooting downward as the victim falls. Most reaches, though, are much

Skyhooks

more active, like an erratic, vigorous, even predominately frantic waving of the arms above the head, a desperate attempt to secure that elusive but ubiquitous skyhook. "Ubiquitous?" you say. Indeed. This reach precedes virtually every bona fide fall. It does not seem to be limited to any race, creed or clime.

Further evidence can be demonstrated by the logger who reaches for this skyhook when his log, on dry land or on water, rolls from under his feet. You see the reach applied with the same confidence in the farmer who misses his step from the high steel deck of his combine fifteen feet up in the air and plunges to the wheat field below. Or the professor, lost deep in philosophical thought, who steps off a three foot curbside, and suddenly minds his matter and reaches as he plunges over the edge. Even the lover boy, gazing at a Beauty as he steps into an open manhole reaches, before his ignoble descent. I could go on. But need I?

I think the evidence is overwhelming. Every human being knows intuitively that there are skyhooks, otherwise why would almost everyone have a natural desire, followed by an immediate response to reach for one?

So, that's the way it was. To this day, anytime I go to fall, I grab for a skyhook. If you had a big brother like mine you probably would too.

Hay Stacking

I was not the most promising prospect for hay stacking. I lacked Bulk. Mashed potatoes, red meat, pounds of spaghetti and Mom's ubiquitous bread had done its part in growing me up, but failed to grow me out. That left me, at five eleven and three quarters inches and one hundred and twenty-five pounds, a bean pole look alike. I had the sinew and the cover, so to speak, to hold my skinny construct together respectfully well, though. I could play basketball and sandlot football well enough to impress the ladies that were over sixty years and under twelve,

Hay Stacking

but I must admit that I lacked a lot of muscle. Charles Atlas was not afraid.

For those putting up hay for winter feed for cattle, horses and such, the process has changed over time. On our farm we just touched the old days of putting up loose hay, that is, not baled by machines in some fashion.

In my hay stacking days, after the baler did the work compacting the hay, it was still picked from the field by hand. A tractor would pull a very low built trailer, a big wooden platform, and one to three stackers would walk along and pick up a bale and set it on the trailer. The one or two men riding on the trailer would pile the bales in a stack on the trailer. When the stack was done, everybody would climb on top and ride it to the barn. There an elevator (a conveyor chain with a motor designed to pull bales high up into a barn to the top of a stack) was set up. One man would unstack the stack on the trailer by taking a bale and placing it on the elevator whereon the bale was drawn up to the stackers who made the permanent stack as storage for winter feed.

Well, often that stack was way up in the haymow in the old barns where loose hay had been stacked in days gone by. The haymow (or room) where the hay was stacked was dimly lit by sunlight sneaking through the hole around the elevator and other sundry holes in the old walls. It could get on the top side of 100 degrees in that stifling atmosphere. The dust and fine hay leaves were so thick that hacking it from the lungs could fill a garden plot with rich soil by the end of the season.

How to Skin a Skunk

We had a '46 Dodge pickup. Dad fashioned a platform that fitted over and a few feet beyond the sides of the pickup bed. He could put it in 'granny gear,' as it was called because in this gear he could set the throttle, a manual pull stop that would hold the engine at just enough gas to keep it going, so the truck would crawl along so slowly even your grandmother could walk beside it and keep up.

Dad would set the throttle and climb out the door to start pitching hay with the pitch fork onto the hay bed while Luisa or Elizabeth and Leo would move it around into a neat stack. The truck would stay pretty much in a straight line, but occasionally one of the older ones would need to steer it a little as it bounced over gopher mounds and ruts. Then Dad, when he could no longer throw the hay high enough, quit pitching, climbed into the truck and drove it from the field to the farmyard to stack in a winter haystack. Along with the older kids he made a big loose haystack west of the house.

We got to dip our hands into the big bags of rock salt and scatter it amongst the hay as they stacked it from off the truck. Why? To cut down the chance of a fire starting by spontaneous combustion. This can happen if the moisture in the hay isn't quite right.

The delicious smell of fresh salted hay tempted us to take it in for dinner for salad, but cows' breath was not appreciated at the table so we settled on chewing salted hay stems as we trampled down the loose hay to make a tight stack.

One evening in the semi-darkness, we boys got to wrestling on a big section of the loose hay, when suddenly Jake let out a

Hay Stacking

scream of pain. As we released whatever hold we had on each other, Jake was writhing about in agony holding his knee. Leo had gotten Jake into a hold that had his arm across the back of Jake's leg and when Jake went over backwards or some such, Leo's arm was where Jake's knee bent and over extended the ligaments in his knee. It ripped a ligament and Mom had to take him to the hospital.

Well anyway, we had a few loose haystacks in the first few years we farmed. I was too little to really help, but I remember it well. There was this special tool that you sawed with both hands called a hay knife. You cut off a section of the stack, the amount you needed that night for feeding the livestock.

The stacking of loose hay was quickly disappearing from the farms when I was young. A machine called a baler compacted the loose hay into bales. Twine or wire kept them together. These were cubes about a foot and a half by two feet by four feet, weighing about sixty to one hundred pounds. The farmer could adjust his machine (the baler) to vary the weight according to whom he knew had to stack them. These were the days when you walked beside a low-slung trailer or truck bed like ours and lifted the bales from the ground and bucked them onto the trailer as it moved along in the field. Long hard work, "bucking bales," and as I entered my teen years I bucked up my fair share. The problem was the bales could weigh in at ninety to one hundred and twenty pounds. I was barely heavier than the bales to be bucked. So it was pert near even-Stephen when they were one hundred pounds.

How to Skin a Skunk

As with most things, Leo set the standard for our work with the farmers around us. His reputation was well deserved and I knew no better hay stacker, both by quantity and quality, and neither did the farmers. He was strong and had prodigious endurance. But what was really neat is he could stack beautifully tight and straight haystacks. Seems silly but it wasn't.

Bales of hay are like big bricks. You have to fit them together just right to keep them even, and more importantly to keep them from collapsing. If the bales aren't stacked correctly, especially at the corners and along the sides, whole sections will collapse out. Many farms' fences and corrals were crushed by these collapsed stacks over the years, not to mention adjacent out buildings and animals. Nope, a good tight stack was essential, and Leo could do that.

One thing that was really quite funny when it did happen: Since no two bales are the exact same size, they would sometimes have gaps between them as they were stacked. The sides of the stack had to be even, perfectly perpendicular to the ground, which would sometimes leave holes near the center of the stack. Holes that the unsuspecting would step in. Every once in a while, two or three gaps would line up, one on top of another from different layers of bales as the stack went up. This would result in a very deep hole.

So there I was one day stacking with a few other guys. These bales averaged one hundred pounds. Those that ran over the average weighed as much as I and even the farmer's son had to ask his dad, who was baling then, to go a little lighter as we

Hay Stacking

would be clean tuckered out and done in before the stack could get from bottom to top.

Well, as I was saying, I was carrying a bale across the stack with its strings, and it hiked up just above my knees. Plum tuckered out, and with great effort, I sputtered to Jeremy, "Sure will be nice to get to the creek for a swi—" Just as I was hitting the "swim," I stepped in a hole and whump, my left leg disappeared into the depths. Down to the hip it went, and the rest of me tried to follow. Well, it couldn't follow so there I was, pinned down, one leg wedged in the most ridiculous angle on top of the bales, the bale I was carrying pinned against my stomach.

I was buried in hay and so skinny, I could barely be seen. In that posture any attempt on my part to extricate myself was quite impossible, and unless someone rescued me I would become cow fodder. I didn't want to be a cow's fodder. I wanted to be a fodder to my own kids one day. I couldn't get any leverage from any angle to move my legs or my arms. Jeremy had noticed the odd way in which my sentence ended and saw me practically disappear from sight. He dropped his bale and grabbed Jake on his way over, and they both grabbed the bale and hurled it off me and pulled me out. They had to act quickly. At the rate Leo stacked and the fact that I was barely thicker than one of the straws, he likely would have stacked right over me and no one would have been the wiser, and my foddering days would have been over before I even got started.

Before the age when we were stackers, back when we were mere salters, Jeremy and I were out hunting one day in the field with our slingshots. We were not far from the hog pens. A big stack of hay had been stacked near the west side of the pens. As we were moving along something made us turn and look. Transfixed, we gaped in horror as one side of the stack let loose of its fellows and toppled sideways like a huge tower falling over, right into the pigpens where the pigs were hamming it up in play.

A sound or shadow alerted the pigs in the nick of time. We watched as the bales left their moorings slowly, then faster, and then with a whoosh of tumbling bales they sped towards and over the pigs who, seeing it, shot like pink streaks across the pen to escape the deluge. A few pigs racing from danger got smacked on the rump by the last of the bales. It took a minute for us to move as the dust cleared. When we could, we looked at each other in utter dismay. Our wide eyed gaze was enough to say, "Did you see that?"

And it did look like total destruction. The remaining stack with its huge gap and the piles of bales strewn all over the pigpen looked like the disaster it was. Fortunately no pigs were hurt.

I remember Dad, Leo and Andy had to restack all that hay. The fence that it had crushed had to be rebuilt. So we had first hand experience of poorly stacked hay and its results. We saw these same results at other farms too.

That's why Leo was in such high demand.

Catching Crawdads

"You get a line; I'll get a pole, honey.
    You get a line; I'll get a pole, baby.
You get a line, and I'll get pole,
We'll go down to the crawdad hole,
Honey, baby mine."

Well that's exactly what Andy and I were doing one hot summer day. We were headed down to our favorite swimming hole in the

How to Skin a Skunk

creek, three miles away by road and two by hiking straight over the Big Hill. My bike was out of order that day so Andy was giving me a ride on his handlebars. He was going to peddle me the whole way like this. Quite an act of heroism, as these were hilly country roads. The creek we were headed to ran under a bridge right before it widened into our swimming hole, and under that bridge was a bed of rocks, and under those rocks were those crawdads we were after.

It's a good time to be warbling when headed to catch crawdads. Only the words had to be a bit modified for our outing; we didn't have poles with us and Andy was certainly not my "baby mine." He was my big brother and if anybody even thought those words referred to him, he'd have leapt off the bike and left me coasting down the road perched in front of the frame of the bike on the handle bars. A ridiculous sight I know, and not without peril to my person, because when that bike knew it could go where it pleased, with no one in the stirrups, it could take me on a ride of its choosing and my disliking. Anyway, no one made Andy leap, so no harm was done.

Arriving safely, we parked our bike and headed for a swim to cool off before we harassed the crawdads. And swum we did. I know, don't tell your folks we swum, they would say there's no such thing as swum, but it was really hot. Usually, it's true, we swam. But this time we just had to swum. Webster couldn't find a crawdad in his book, so maybe he left swum on the table among his word scraps and never got it glued back in.

After we were done with our swum, we waded up the creek until we were under the bridge.

Catching Crawdads

The crawdads were no fools. They had chosen these rocks under the bridge as their lair, as these rocks had particular charms about them that made great fortresses against marauding boys. These rocks were anywhere from golf ball size to basketball size but so much more. It's as if they had been chipped from some rock cliff and come off in sharp sided angles. They were jumbled all over one another under the bridge.

The idea was to enter into this underwater world of rocks and crawdads by wading into it, bending down, and then turning the rocks over to expose shy creatures underneath. Then when a crawdad was spotted that was foolish enough not to scurry under another rock, you could slowly reach down, put your hand into the water, lower it until you got really close, and then thrust your hand down and pin him against the stream bed right behind his head, just far enough back on his hard shelled back that his huge pinchers couldn't reach back and take a chunk of your finger out.

Huge wooden beams spanned the creek and supported the bridge that we were under. Girders, I think they're called. This rough cut lumber made perfect imitation cliffs for the swallows, where they would build their mud nests. Hundreds of them flying in, under, and out from under the bridge to feed their young or dive bomb us. The beams were only about four feet above our heads, so the musical notes of the swallows enveloped our little cave like a world under the bridge as they cavorted around chittering and chattering to their mates and babies.

We looked like crooked up scarecrows as we gingerly placed our feet amongst the rocks and waved our arms around trying to keep our balance. The current pushed us a bit as it roiled around the rocks and our shins. It was nice and clear water, from one to two feet deep.

The crawdads were no pushovers. They had a few defenses in place. One was a fine slippery substance coated all over the rocks, a very thin layer of moss that grew on them. Greenish brown in color, it coated everything under water. I could just imagine the crawdads painting this all over the rocks. A liberal slathering would do. Then they would watch from their little lairs, gleefully, a little evilly, until a boy would stand on a rare smooth rock where he thought he could put all his weight down without cutting himself on a jagged edge. Then through the beady little eyes of the crawdad, he would watch the boy put his weight down with a satisfied look and WHOOPS! His foot would shoot forward on the slippery sheen and run his toes into a huge boulder and out from his mouth would escape a most piercing scream of pain. The scream seemed to work equally well if he managed to keep his balance or if he went over on his back. A gurgle at the end let you know, though, which, and added a little flair when the result was flat-on-your-back.

The scream had consequences. The crawdads didn't seem picky as to whether the left foot or the right was offended. They would arrange a few rocks such that as your foot shot forward it disappeared in a small cave or crevice and this thrust would implant your toes on the next hidden rock, scrunching them together and then smashing them. The scream of pain that followed would crumble the mud nest, hatch the eggs prematurely, pop nestlings from their beds of down, and generally shatter the

Catching Crawdads

swallow world. A crawdad dance would then commence, and the boys that still had their toes in normal proportion would go into convulsions of laughter.

How did I know these crawdads did this on purpose? That their tiny little brains were intelligent? Well, the traps were just too perfect. And when that much design is manifest, you know there is intelligence, although perhaps some modern architects or clothing designers belie this otherwise universal truth.

Well anyway, crawdads don't wear clothes, and I was never in the mood to lend them mine.

That mean business above was the first way a crawdad defended his kingdom. The second way was when you got up close and personal. Crawdads back up. Fast. Yep, that's what they do. By nature. But don't conclude they're cowards. They are just maneuvering into position to get their claws ready to pinch you. Hard. And this pinch can leave a nasty cut. Usually when you surprise them into sight, they back up quickly into another crevice or cave. But sometimes they freeze and stay motionless, and that's when you lower your hand to grab them. Since they're so quick at backing, when you lunge they back up, and whereas you're supposed to grab them on their hard shelled back, you grab now right on the neck, and there they have you because they can reach back and grab your finger. And YEEOUCH!!

I saw a kid once, well not that kind. Goats aren't really into crawdad fishing, but I saw a boy who was bested and he had blood flowing from his fingers to prove it. Lots of blood. Rivers of it. Well not rivers, but a creek. Well not the whole creek. It didn't really run with blood, but the boy bellowed like it did, and it was flowing. Well. Both were, the blood and the creek. And in this story, I guess, we'd better stop the flow, before we lose the boy.

There was one more weapon these crawdads used to ambush the weary boy. Cackleberry thorns. Remember, those bushes lined the creek banks. They grew easily inch long thorns, hard as nails and needle sharp. These, the crawdads placed strategically around the creek bottom. It looked haphazard if you could see them but mostly you couldn't. A branch with these thorns would be lying on the creek bottom, slimed with moss, so well camouflaged your peds were in clear and present danger.

And sure enough this time, as we were just entering the large rocks under the bridge, still gingerly picking our way along the sharp rocks that littered the creek floor before it emptied into the sandy pond, I let out an OW, OW, OW! Because my big toe, feeling around adventurously, had, without my permission orally or in writing, placed itself over a thorn. I, putting my full faith and assent on the placing of my foot *down*, did so. And that thorn pierced my big toe, and continued its impertinence until it had imbedded its whole length into my toe and perhaps all the way to my larynx, because although I felt it in my toe it was my voice that objected and let the world know. So there I danced on my left foot all over sharp rocks as I held my right foot in my right hand. I yodeled and yelped, howled and yowled, and perhaps even yapped, reached with my left hand and yanked out the offending thorn. With a whimper I ended this one legged

Catching Crawdads

dance, stretched my foot into the cool creek water and soothed my pokered toe.

So don't go feeling sorry for these crawdads unless perhaps for a Catholic crawdad that wasn't allowed to eat meat on Fridays and so was forbidden to pinch us on those days.

We caught some but didn't keep any. It was just fun to best them a few times. We'd wave them around in the air and yell, "I got one!" and compare them. Then we would throw them back.

Tired of this, we'd position ourselves on our fannies and let the creek current push our backs, and we'd bounce and slide down the slick rocks until we were pushed into the mouth of the pond that made our swimming hole. And then, a little swimming before heading home.

And somewhere over the rainbow, or something like that, a little infant girl, Clarabelle, heard a very faint "Baby Mine" waft over the Cascade Mountains to the west as we coasted down the driveway towards the house, where sat around the table the pleasantest populace one could have. We did not, however sit down to a crawdad supper. Only a few brave souls once tried cooked crawdads. All I remember is they tasted like chicken flavored mud. It wasn't anymore successful than our cooked crow. The family clearly preferred to hear us talk of crawdad tales than eat them. So we regaled the table with tales of crawdads that evening until someone yelled "The cows are out!"

I looked all over in Webster's big book of words to find a crawdad when I began to write this tale. I could not find even one crawdad. Got curious to see if Merriam had ever had one, so I looked in his collection of words and no, not even an honorable mention in his Dictionary.

I did find crayfish. Oh, yes, crayfish seemed to crawl all over the pages. They even got their pictures taken and posted right there on page 442, but not a mention of crawdads. The crayfish looked exactly like crawdads. They aped them in every way. One would even think that they were the same thing. But I know we caught crawdads. Leo and Andy called them crawdads and that authority is virtually unassailable.

The locals called them crawdads and there is a quite popular folk song called the Crawdad Song and I'll set down my pen right now and let the ink go dry if I don't count nineteen times crawdads are pointed out, and twenty even, if you count the title. Now you'll have to rosin up your larynx and yodel through all ten verses yourself if you doubt me, but I just mention the following incontrovertible facts stated in the refrain:

He got a line and she got a pole and they went down to the *crawdad* hole and I just can't imagine a real romancer going down to a crayfish hole. Doesn't sound right. She'll never have it. And besides, the nomenclature has the stamp of official approval by the government no less, because in verse five, it says the crawdad: crawling around was the mayor of Crawdad Town. And mayors are official government property. So I ask you: Would the government allow the mayor to be a mayor under false pretenses? So it couldn't have been a crayfish.

Catching Crawdads

And that was a very important point to get settled before you dive in for another grab at a crawdad. You go diving in confused and you'll git bit.

Apparently there are whole sections of the country where crawdads are masquerading as crayfish. It's a crawdad trap. They will get these kids to think they are going crayfish catching, and then maybe even convince them that they have rubber lips or something and then in just the old crawdad way, what will they do? Pinch.

Both Merriam and Webster fell for it. Just goes to show you can't believe everything you read. You do read don't you?

Climbing Trees

I climbed trees, we climbed trees, you probably climbed trees, and you may even have clumb some trees before grammar got a hold of you. Either way, tree climbing seems to be a pretty well established institution, having roots well before I was out of the nest and continuing now as we and the trees grow into maturity.

Some Fir, a few Lodge Pole, a Tamarack tree here and there, but mostly Ponderosa wooded the west side of our property. They

Climbing Trees

had the old mine well surrounded. And in those trees we built forts, played Cowboys and Indians, and of course climbed a lot.

We had all staked out our favorite climbing trees. Mine was a large trunked Ponderosa pine that was only twenty feet or so into the woods from our fence line. A sort of mutant branch had grown far too large from the trunk about fifteen feet off the ground. It was a good foot in diameter where it met the trunk, and had grown so long and heavy that it broke; but not off. After the break, the branch swept down to only a few feet from the ground where we could sit on it and make it sway up and down. Where the big crack was when it broke from the trunk there was a level piece of wood where I could put the carcasses of the varied feathered and furred animals I had conked out with my sling shot. There the carnivorous beetles and many other undertakers would reduce them to mere bones, which I gathered for my skeleton collection.

The really neat thing was that you could half run, half climb this huge sweeping branch from the ground all the way up to the tree trunk. The rest of the tree from the break was there to go up as high as you wanted. This one, and most of the trees around, were probably one hundred feet tall or so. I only climbed all the way to the top once or twice. I was just not one for heights. Jeremy and Jake did it a number of times. They would go all the way until the trunk became too thin and the branches were too little to go higher.

Well, one day I was determined to do anything necessary to get a young Magpie for a pet. This is before I realized that Magpies much preferred the thorny Cackleberry bushes along the creek beds to pine trees. Rarely did they nest in trees. Happened though that I did detect a Magpie frequenting a place way up in one of the pine trees, and I determined I was going to find its nest up there.

So I began to clumb. I hadn't gotten very far up when Noah Webster caught up to me and demanded I stop clumbing as there is no such thing as clumbing up a tree. First time I'd heard this. I'd been asked many times how many trees I'd clumb and I, in my wisdom, just told on myself. Fancy he telling me there is no such thing as clumbing on my way up my Magpie tree. I almost fell out in alarm, but luckily I hung on and started climbing before I got hurt. So I climbed, and I climbed some more until I realized I had clumb (climbed!) nearly to the top. Well there was a nest, and I thought it was a Magpie nest, but I doubt it now. What I do remember is getting a little shaky, for I had been concentrating on climbing, as the branches were pretty thick, and I hadn't looked out away from the tree until now. And when I did ... what a sight!

I could see way over our farmstead and way across the pastures and fields for what seemed like forever, and a little shiver of pre-panic shook me as it dawned on me that I was way, way up. And it was a long, long way down, and it was very, very hard ground. As I took another look, I saw way, way off, so far north in fact, that a little piece of southern Alaska came into view, and this view was so far away that it was a bit hazy, perhaps eight hundred miles away or so, and about eight years into the future. There I saw another boy (young man perhaps, but still me), way up in a tree, looking way, way down. And there, coming into focus, for me and I hope for you, is the singing logger. Yep, that's me.

Climbing Trees

I know, I know. Singing logger just doesn't have any poetry to it. Singing cowboy does, everybody just gushes about them. There are the yodeling ones, the crooners, the balladeers, and the rhinestones: hundreds of them serenading the fruited plains making gazillions of dollars, those singing cowboys. Well, it wasn't a cowboy.

You are aware I was scared of heights; really scared of heights. Not just a little. So scared of heights that just to say the word sort of makes me weak in the knees.

So now you're asking, "Just what are you doing sixty feet up in a tree?" (Remember, we're eight years ahead of where we were in that pine tree above). "Don't loggers cut down trees and put them on their shoulders and shinny them off the hillsides?" Well, that's how Paul Bunyan and our Wisconsin cousin loggers did it. Paul Bunyan, the famous logger I'm sure you've read about. Well, I was a logger like him and was sure to be logged in the annals of logger lore, but he crowded me out. He had a blue ox and I didn't.

Perhaps if I had a purple cow I would have eclipsed his reputation. Regrettably, I didn't have a purple cow and Gelett Burgess didn't want to be one as he stated quite emphatically:

> I never saw a Purple Cow,
> I never hope to see one,
> But I can tell you anyhow,
> I'd rather see than be one!

How to Skin a Skunk

Well did he see one? I could sure have used one if he did. But swaying around up in that tree was not the time to reflect upon this "might have been" and Gelett seemed a bit touchy about me mentioning it anyway.

In his own words, no less:

> Ah yes, I wrote the Purple Cow
> I am sorry now I wrote it!
> But I can tell you anyhow
> I'll kill you if you quote it!

So I didn't have a purple cow.

Now to understand why I was up in the tree you have to understand just a few things about the kind of logging we were doing.

On the steep hillside, in what is called "high lead logging operations" there was, in this basic pecking order: Side Rod, Hook Tender, Riggin Slinger, Chaser and Choker Setters. Wedged in there was a guy called a Second Rigger. He was the helper and mule for the Hook Tender. You see? Yep. All clear. Now I know all these words make perfect sense to you. Just a warning though. Don't call a shackle a clevis, a block a pulley or a line a cable, and never ask what's a henway. You'll be called a farmer in derision until you out logger or out slaughter them.

You notice I mentioned blocks. For most of you this is known as a pulley. It would be too lengthy in this tale to explain how

Climbing Trees

the whole operation worked. For one thing I want to get down out of this tree as soon as I can.

There were pulleys a Hook Tender and Second Rigger moved at least twice a day and sometimes a lot more. Four were being set up as the loggers cleaned the logs from under the lines that were strung through the pulleys the two of you had just set up. When they finished, the lines were re-strung through the new four pulley layout and the former were then moved past the present operation and set for the next run. These pulleys were attached either to stumps as anchors or way up in a tree as a lift to the lines. They were attached by lines (cables) called straps. Now the block (pulley) that attached to the straps weighed eighty pounds, and the ones hung in the lift trees were sixty pounds a piece. The straps for the eighty pounders weighed forty-five pounds and the straps for the sixty pounders, thirty.

These all had to be carried by hand from one place to the other. There was a technique acquired, after a time, to hoist the block onto your shoulders to carry it. Then you usually dragged the strap along, although sometimes you had to coil it and carry it too. Now, that's a lot of weight to be trucking around, especially in the Southeastern Alaska Inland Forest. Up steep hillsides, clambering over mossy fallen logs, sliding down steep slopes in Devil's Club thorns, and trying to avoid being swallowed in the Muskeg swamps. Considering the average weight of a logger was anywhere from one hundred and sixty five to two hundred and twenty five pounds, and I checked in at the beginning of the seasons at about one hundred and twenty-six and bulked up to a whopping one hundred and fifty-five by the end, it was a real challenge for me.

Well, I was up in that tree getting the blocks and straps out.

Now just wait a minute! How did the hook tender carry those blocks up a tree? Sixty pounds on his back, a thirty pound strap and sometimes no branches and sometimes thick branches. How'd he do it?

Well, they weren't clumb like that. He didn't use branches to climb at all. The kind of climbing he did used special spurs attached to his legs and over his boots.

Some of you may have seen linemen for the power companies wear climbing gear like that. First there were some leather straps that were fastened around the lower leg. On these straps was a steel spur that hung down from the arch of the boot. A spur was strapped on each foot. Then you put this belt harness around your waist which had a big metal ring on it, snug up by your right waist.

There was a thick rope attached to the belt on your left waist. Stepping up to the tree you wished to climb you slung the rope with your left hand around the tree and grabbed it with your right as it came whipping around. On thin trees you had to be careful it didn't come around and slap you on the back of the head. Having grabbed the rope with your right hand, you slipped it through the metal ring and tied a special knot to keep it snug.

Now if the knot was naught what it was supposed to be, and you were sixty feet up in the air where you ought, and that knot un-knotted when it ought not, you would take a mighty fall to the forest floor where, splattled, your immortal self might be

Climbing Trees

a lot farther down, where it's very hot, unless perhaps you had sought a lot where it is not hot.

Well, after you got your knot knotted, then up the tree you stepped, much like going up stairs. Stab your spur on the right and push up and then stab your spur on the left a foot or so up the tree and back to the right and up you go.

You had to flip that rope that you slung in a special way so that it climbed the tree on the back side from you as you went up. That rope kept you from falling backwards off the tree, and when you got tired you just kept your spurs dug in and leaned back against this rope for a breather. You see, you depend a lot on that knot. Funny little thing happens, though, as you get higher and higher. The tree diameters get smaller and smaller and your rope gets looser and looser around the tree as the loop gets bigger and bigger in comparison to the diameter of the trunk. So now the rope loop is too big and sags down too far on the backside and you could be toppled over backwards.

What to do? Well, you untie that critical knot holding you up there and retie it after pulling the slack in the rope through the ring farther. You can't let a spur slip out or lean back on the rope when the knot is loose or down you go a whole lot faster than you went up!

So, I'm scared of heights, and here I am forty-five feet or so up and getting a little trembly. I look up and there is the block another fifteen feet up! Fifteen feet! I have to loosen the knot again and take up more slack. I don't want to. I don't see how I can go up that last fifteen feet. But I dig in deep and do it.

How to Skin a Skunk

Then I did the unforgivable. I looked down. The trunk looked a little skinnier down there than when I started up. It looked a long way down, and I still had to go up. So I started up again and my nerves began to fail so I did something, anything to distract myself from the reality of what I was doing. There's not a lot of options up there. You can't go skating in a buffalo herd, you can't pause and chat with the bark beetles or chew the fat with Aunt Sally. You really only have two options: Go up, young man, go up, for you and your dignity; or down, down to dollarlessness and shame.

So I did what I could. I sang. I sang loud and lustily. My lungs filled with pure Alaskan air and expelled in hearty verse.

"Glory, Glory, Hallelujah," I belted out with all my might as I spurred up another step. "His truth is marching on," I yelled to the sky as the other spur kicked in another foot up.

Need more height.

"Mine eyes have seen the glory of the coming of the Lord." I felt I was certainly high enough to see Him face to face. The heavens were getting closer as I moved up a couple more feet. I began to falter. "I can't do this," a little voice sounded in my soul. "He has sounded forth His trumpet that shall never call retreat," I holler-sang in defiance to the trees around me. I shall not retreat and I gained a few more feet.

My forearms were now looking a lot like Popeye's, pumped full of blood as I about squeezed my rope in two. I could see the bell and nubbin that I had to reach there above my head. "Just too far," I was tempted again. "Come on lungs, more air," and with that I sucked with all my might and I let out, "He is sifting out the heart of men before His judgment seat," and now even the bark beetles were getting religion, and I had to ask: "Was I a coward or a man?" The judgment awaited me. "Coward!" every sinew of my body screamed. But I stepped higher, and there, almost at my forehead was that infernal bell. "Oh, be swift my soul to answer Him." My soul said yes! "Be jubilant my feet." They surged with joy and gave me that last step up.

The bell and nubbin were now at my chest. I was sweating profusely and had to sing more quietly as I concentrated on snapping the nubbin from the bell and dropping it, snaking, to the ground. Oh, what a relief! I could go down now.

The intensity of the emotion subsided gradually as I neared the ground, there to take the climbing gear off and pack the block and strap to the next tree, where the Hook Tender would climb and place them.

And then up another tree I would go. And somewhere up in the heights I would start singing again. I didn't always need the spiritual. Sometimes just a good old fashioned ballad would do, and I would press into service my darling Clementine.

"Oh my darling, oh my darling," would get me up a few steps. Add the beautiful name Clemintine and more height was achieved.

"Oh my darling, oh my darling Clementine," I wailed. "You were lost and gone forever..."

Did I really need to be reminded what would happen to me if I slipped out of that tree? No, not that, so I shouted out another verse to stiffen my spine. And it did. By now I was really in love with this girl. Hadn't met her father miner yet, but she swelled my heart as I climbed, clumb, and sung. Oh yes, I sung, and I sung and I sunged until my sunger was sore. But I still had to go up more. So I plaintively implored again, "Oh my darling, Clementine" and with that I reached the bell and nubbin and in jubilation I sang some more and, oops, she goes and falls into the brine and leaves me.

Brine is fine, makes a real good jerky, but how could I go diving in to save Clementine from way up here? All I could see was a muskeg swamp. Besides, I didn't even know her all that well. I only had met her at the beginning of the song and my love had only grown up with one tree, and here I already lost her before the end of the song.

It was a short love affair as I was swaying there in the tree tops. But it helped to conquer my fear, climb the company's tree and keep my dignity. Clementine and I renewed our acquaintance many times up in the tree tops when I needed a spark, but she never could stop falling into the brine. To have and to hold she couldn't, so I had to wait until Clarabelle to have and hold to make me bold.

There was a bit of talk around the camps about a man who sang in the treetops of Alaska. And maybe, just maybe, one day in the concert hall, the lights will come on and there, not a singing cowboy, but the one and only singing logger will emerge.

But oh! I am still up in this Magpie tree, and I'd better get down. Now what about that tree, an owl's nest perhaps? Owlets?... Better wait for next time!